CASHING IN ON WALL STREET'S TEN GREATEST MYTHS

CASHING IN ON WALL STREET'S TEN GREATEST MYTHS

What You Can Do to
Consistently Build Wealth

Richard L. Lackey

McGRAW-HILL
New York Chicago San Francisco Lisbon
London Madrid Mexico City Milan New Delhi
San Juan Seoul Singapore Sydney Toronto

The **McGraw·Hill** Companies

1 2 3 4 5 6 7 8 9 0 DOC/DOC 0 9 8 7 6 5 4

ISBN 0-07-144488-2

This publication is designed to provide accurate and authoritative information in regard to the subject matter covered. It is sold with the understanding that the publisher is not engaged in rendering legal, accounting, or other professional service. If legal advice or other expert assistance is required, the services of a competent professional person should be sought.—*From a declaration of principles jointly adopted by a committee of the American Bar Association and a committee of publishers.*

McGraw-Hill books are available at special discounts to use as premiums and sales promotions, or for use in corporate training programs. For more information, please write to the Director of Special Sales, Professional Publishing, McGraw-Hill, Two Penn Plaza, New York, NY 10121-2298. Or contact your local bookstore.

 This book is printed on recycled, acid-free paper containing a minimum of 50% recycled de-inked paper.

Library of Congress Cataloging-in-Publication Data

Lackey, Richard L.
  Cashing in on Wall Street's 10 greatest myths : what you can do to consistently build wealth / by Richard L. Lackey.
    p. cm.
  ISBN 0-07-144488-2 (hardcover : alk. paper)
  1. Portfolio management. 2. Investments. 3. Stocks. 4. Wealth. 5. Finance, Personal. I. Title.
  HG4529.5.L33 2004
  332.6—dc22   2004015436

Contents

Preface

What is it about investing that makes it both exciting and frightening? In talking to investors of all ages and from very diverse backgrounds for more than two decades, I have found that only one thing separates the investor who approaches the market with trepidation and the one who approaches it with confidence. That thing is knowledge. I don't mean just the knowledge that comes from reading a book like this. I mean the knowledge that comes from questioning the logic of market gurus and pundits, and the knowledge that is derived from seeing good ideas fail and bad ideas succeed. I mean the knowledge that arises from a true appreciation for the immense opportunity that is available to the salient investor.

Whether done properly or improperly, investing is often the one thing that has the most profound effect on our financial future. To a large degree we are always investing—our time, our effort, and our emotions. When we are able to manage these things efficiently, we tend to be at our best. The perspective we use to filter our judgment colors all that we do in life. As it pertains to our financial lives, our perspective drives our approach to investing and directs the efforts we take to achieve our goals. It is remarkable how little time is dedicated to ensuring the success of such a vital aspect of our lives. Those who treat their investments like orchids, learning how they best grow and tending to them regularly, find that in time they seem to grow rapidly with very little attendance. My goal in writing this book is to share with you a perspective on investing that has proved successful for savvy investors around the globe for many decades.

After more than 20 years of study in the martial arts, I have come to some realizations that have proved to be as pertinent in investing as they are in the ring. One of these truths is that if you intend to last, you must have a good defense. You can never know exactly what the future has in store. There will always be an unexpected blow. Most likely there will be several unexpected blows. For investors, it is a global depression that is made worse by the fraudulent actions of CEOs and the inexplicable massacre of thousands of innocent citizens. This brings us to the second truth. Not everyone uses the same standards of logic. If this were the case, there would be no need for multiple political parties, and wars would cease to exist. This disparity is what makes us human, though it often seems we border on the inhumane.

Over time, economies soar and economies crash. There is no reason for anyone to suffer the loss of his or her life savings because of economic downturns. What we need is to recognize that the financial models hundreds of millions have invested in for decades are flawed. They have never been correct, and yet the multiple times that these theories have revealed the extent of their ineffective nature, they have been met with passivity. While those who have adopted a more practical approach to the markets and to the management of risk have fared well, the rest of Wall Street has not learned anything and has continued once again on its merry way. Time and time again the overwhelming proof for actively managing risk has been established. Sadly, the shock of the recent bear market has served once again to alert the buy-and-hold investor of a need for change.

This book is not intended to be a treatise on the maladies or malfeasance of the financial industry. On the contrary, it is intended to clarify where real opportunity lies and where it does not. Most importantly, I hope that the ideas shared here stimulate you to take action—not to change your broker or buy a certain stock or mutual fund, but rather to establish your own well-defined investing philosophy. If you know what you believe, then you can more effectively determine what you expect to achieve. This may mean approaching your investments from a new direction. The hope is that it will include a paradigm shift accompanied by a more enlightened market view.

Acknowledgments

Thank you to my friends, family, and colleagues who shared their time and energy so that this effort might be fruitful. I owe much to the thousands of traders and investors whose honest concern made clear the need for a shift in the investor paradigm. In my work, I could not ask for greater friends and colleagues than Pat Downing, whose commonsense approach to business is continuously refreshing; and Terry Cartrite, whose wisdom and faith keep our organization focused; and especially Scott Thompson, whose passion is enough to keep everyone going. I have been blessed with more than business partners. I have been given great friends.

Meera Goel, in addition to being a wonderful friend of the entire family, played a significant part in helping me to organize many of the ideas and concepts shared in the text.

The motivation to complete this book was generated by the wonderful Stephen Isaacs of McGraw-Hill, whom I am honored to have publishing this book.

Thanks to my mother for her love and support over the years, and most importantly for her unwavering faith in my brother and me. Whether we were skydiving or mountain climbing, she has always urged us to do our best and seek our highest potential. I am also indebted to my father for his starting me on my trek into the world of finance more than a quarter century ago. My grandmother, Nonnie, whose smile never fails to warm the hearts of those around her, taught me that common sense is more valuable than gold.

And for the abundant wealth that I enjoy every day, I thank the Lord for my amazing and brilliant wife, Paige, and my beautiful and talented children, Sydney and Ansley. They are more than I deserve and certainly more than I could ever have imagined.

Introduction

In *Cashing in on Wall Street's Ten Greatest Myths*, we examine the myths and misconceptions that have been exploited by Wall Street to the ruin of millions. Each myth can be studied and appreciated independently to reveal its onerous nature and its inherently negative impact on long-term investor profitability, but there is greater value to be found when the subject matter is considered in aggregate. Either way, the picture clearly depicts a Wall Street that has been herding investors like bulls in Pamplona. As an investing public we have been duped by bad science and Wall Street wire houses that have put corporate profits above the fiduciary responsibility they are supposed to uphold. Through a simple appreciation for what is the true nature of the financial markets, investors can learn to reduce risk while enjoying wonderful returns over time.

The assumption that risk is diametrically opposed to reward is the first stepping-stone laid by Wall Street in its road to perdition. By all accounts, risk and reward are related in most investments, but only in rare cases is their relationship one that is truly opposite. It may not sound important, but it matters tremendously when you compare investment alternatives. In fact, if this were not the case, there would be little difference between investing in the financial markets and spinning your money away at a roulette wheel. This myth has becomes so pervasive that an entire class of investors now treat their brokerage account like a virtual casino.

Only two decades ago broker-dealers made much of their money charging sizable commissions and earning the "spread" (the difference between the bid price and the ask price of a security). I remember purchasing one stock in the early 1980s that had a $5 spread. The bid price, or what the market was willing to pay for the stock, was $51 per share, while the ask price, or the price at which the market was offering the stock for sale, was $56 per share. Because my broker "liked me," I was able to buy 1000 shares at the bargain price of $55 per share (a dollar below the ask). One week later new information turned up that I interpreted as negative, and so I called my broker to sell the stock. Ironically the bid price for the stock was still $51 per share, and the ask price had remained at $56 per share. Again, my broker got me a better price than the bid, and I was able to sell my 1000 shares for $52 a share. When you consider that there was also a $180 commission charge when I bought the stock and a $180 commission charge on the sale of the stock, the total cost for entering and exiting the trade of this stagnant stock was $3360 ($3 per share × 1000 shares + $360 in commission expense), or 13.7 percent. The cost to do business was so high that any strategy other than buy and hold was often considered an exercise in futility. Wall Street, during this era, was well delineated from the likes of Las Vegas and Monte Carlo. Profits were not meant to be had swiftly, but rather they were to be earned over time. Consequently, when to buy seemed important, however, when to sell was rarely mentioned. Even the concept of managing risk by using a strategy as simple as a stop-loss order was regarded as a futile effort to control the uncontrollable. Whether by default or by design, the mantra was unequivocally "buy and hold."

But as the wealth of the citizenry grew, so did the interest in the financial markets. In the late 1980s and early 1990s, discount brokerage firms began popping up everywhere. Low commissions and electronic access to the markets were empowering to the individual investor. The rush to online trading quickly put pressure on Wall Street's most established firms, forcing them to provide similar access to the markets along with more favorable commission structures.

Value investing took on an entirely new look. Valuation models that were the standard for a century prior were being tossed out the window. To keep up, the largest firms relied on the insight of market-savvy analysts to find the next big winner for the investing public. Analysts went from back-office researchers to prime-time superstars on television and radio and in print. Instead of breaking down the fundamental earning capacity of a firm to arrive at a fair valuation, analysts reverted to the relative valuation of one company to its peers. Those who said they would never use any form of technical analysis quickly adopted new criteria for their fundamental analysis that by classical standards were outrageous. The public now knows to be true what was suspected by many industry insiders: that the end can always justify the means.

Wall Street continued to preach its mantra of buy and hold, but with a twist. The push was to buy more and hold more. And it worked. Investors who took on the latest and greatest companies were well rewarded; and those on margin were really well rewarded. In fact, a little margin and some moderately aggressive stock picking allowed the prosperity to flow like ouzo at a Greek wedding. Analysts and fund managers were rewarded with hefty bonuses for their stellar performance; and more investors became overnight millionaires than at any other time in history.

But companies could not sustain their astronomical valuations forever, and so like Icarus falling after flying too close to the sun, the market tumbled down. Scared brokers and unprepared investors retreated into the quiet recesses of their new beach homes, wishing, hoping, and praying. They sought comfort in repeating those fateful words: "Buy and hold. I must buy and hold!" Millions bought more as the markets continued to crumble, certain that they would bounce back soon. Millions more just held their positions, watching their equity wither away.

And so the markets had turned, as markets on occasion do. Mutual fund managers began selling their stocks that were rocketing downward to fund the purchase of other stocks that were merely plummeting. For more than two years those fund managers who were successful in losing only 40 percent of their net asset value were rewarded for losing less than the market. The concept of paying for performance as it compares with a benchmark has emerged from the misconception that somehow relative performance should be valued more than the absolute net return. Common sense tells us that the outlook for retirement does not improve when our accounts lose 40 percent of their value. When mutual funds or investment advisers compare their performance with benchmarks like the Dow (Dow Jones Industrial Average) or the S&P 500 (Standard & Poor's select group of 500 large-capitalization firms), they are in essence telling the investor that he or she has little hope of really outperforming the market over time, and as such should be satisfied with any improvement over the index averages. Wall Street would have you believe that there is some glimmer of hope, perhaps some small chance that with good research and careful stock selection we as investors might find stocks that will do better than the indexes, but we must be patient enough to buy and hold. I certainly don't want my future tied to any market, and I hope you don't either. The markets are only tools for building wealth, but their intrinsic movement should never define what measure of wealth one should obtain over time.

The dynamic nature of the financial markets is not to be taken lightly. Though a graph of the major market indexes reveals a general trend upward over the past 200 years, most of us do not invest for more than 40 or 50 years before we begin to draw on our investments for retirement. When we look at graphs of the financial markets over more realistic time horizons, we find that the volatility increases geometrically. This is one reason that so many people who were investing for the 30 years prior to the recent market crash were ruined. Markets hold no regard for an individual's long-term investment goals, and those who pursue investments that cannot survive during extended bear markets put themselves unduly in harm's way.

Mutual funds, commonly considered a safe and appropriate vehicle for those seeking long-term portfolio growth, have generally proved to perform no better than passive index funds. In theory, mutual funds should provide a method for investors to obtain real diversification in a particular market, industry, or sector with the benefits of active and expert management. But, in reality, the world of mutual funds is plagued by mandates to buy and hold. The ability for mutual fund managers to truly engage in active management is greatly exaggerated.

Consequently, everyday investors spurned by the mendacity of Wall Street are now joining forces with those who regard hedge funds and the like as the new gold standard. The reason this paradigm shift is so important is that it is compelling investment advisers, broker-dealers, financial planners, and even government regulators to reconsider established guidelines. Those who are already active in this introspective effort have quickly come to the conclusion that there is a need for real and massive change.

The political palaver that has historically surrounded most attempts to improve the plight of the average investor and the small retirement plan administrator has generally been peppered with references to the lack of proper investor sophistication. This is almost laughable when we consider the less than stellar performance of the institutions that promote the passive buy-and-hold approach to investing; and yet they refuse to change. If their sophisticated approach does no better than it has, then maybe it's more than just the sophistication—maybe it's the approach. Thankfully, we live in a capitalist society where supply and demand have great impact on the market. I expect that within the next dozen years those asset classes that are now considered alternative will be the bricks and mortar of the investment world, while the mutual funds of today will simply be used to fill in the cracks. As the average investor evolves in his or her understanding and appreciation of the opportunities that exist, Wall Street will not be able to hide the way it has in the past. If you know where to look, you can get on this train long before it leaves the station

The IPO, or initial public offering, is just one of the unique areas for prospecting in the financial markets. Outside of creating or running your own business, there is little excitement in the world of finance that compares to being part of a company going public. In the eighties and nineties every company seemed poised to take advantage of some new burgeoning market; and every major market-making firm wanted to be part of the process. However, the Wall Street myth that IPOs are easy money is just factually untrue. A lot goes into finding great IPOs, and much of it is not readily available. Wall Street has little motivation for educating investors on the intricacies of IPO investing. Though there is not a lot of noise being made now about IPOs, there is always a treasure to be found if you know where to dig. We will discuss in detail the techniques used by industry experts to separate the pyrite from the profits.

Where IPOs may carry more risk than you might think without the proper research, options can enhance both the safety and performance of your portfolio with less effort and risk than you might think. Options and other derivative products such as financial and commodity futures recognize leverage as an integral part of their design. For the buy-and-hold crowd, leverage can only amplify the inherently severe swings; but for the rest of us, leverage is just another device for achieving our goals. Like the proponents of big government, the advocates of buy and hold assume that average citizens would be better off letting someone else take care of them. Just the suggestion that people are not capable of understanding something as simple as the options market is an insult.

The other myth contrived by Wall Street is that options are only for the extreme risk takers. What hogwash. I have met 85- and 90-year-old retirees who use options regularly to hedge their portfolios and to increase their cash flow. They are far too conservative to sit and watch their portfolios rise and fall like everyone else. They don't perceive their investing time line to be 70 years, much less 200 years.

Most brokers don't recommend option strategies to their clients for one reason: they have never taken the time to learn them. It is difficult at best to incorporate effective strategies that you know nothing about. Moreover, brokerage firms recognize that there is less commission to be had in selling options than in selling mutual funds; and options require that the broker be proactive in his or her management of the client's account. This translates into less time being available for the broker to cold-call prospects. I am going to share with you a few of my favorite strategies for building wealth with options later in the book. The techniques are time tested and have proved effective. That is far more than can be said about much of the theory that has been taught to your average broker.

Logic has never been a requirement for much of anything, but it affects almost everything. Likewise, most brokers are not pusillanimous creatures with ill intent; they have just been accepting of fatuous logic that has propped up the financial models that are considered standard in the industry. The concept of diversification is a perfect example. Modern Portfolio Theory was introduced by Harry Markowitz, who later won a Nobel Prize for his work. From Modern Portfolio Theory came the Efficient Frontier Hypothesis, which considers a universe of risky investments and explores what might be an optimal portfolio based upon those possible investments. When clients are shown where their most lucrative blend of investments lies on the efficient frontier, they are generally not privy to the universe from which the selection is based. Accordingly, the decisions made are often reflective of the ideal portfolio mix based on the products available through the financial planner and not necessarily on the products that would best fit the needs of the investor.

Additionally, the general asset allocation model endorsed by brokers is regularly based on the false assumption that what was appropriate in 1952 still holds true today. This is almost always *not* the case. For example, investing internationally was considered a great way to gain diversification 40 years ago, but every decade since, the world has grown closer together. Where European and Asian markets were in many cases inversely correlated with U.S. markets, they are now almost 80 percent correlated. This means that by simply spreading our equity investments abroad, we gain very little intrinsic diversification.

The bond market is another perfect example. The significance of bonds in a diversified portfolio was first considered valuable as an asset class whose price performance was converse to that of the stock market. Now, however, bonds regularly move in sympathy with equities.

So, although the theories themselves have merit, their application has been anything but straightforward. Each of these missteps can prove devastating to the long-term investor. Diversification in the wrong hands serves not only to dilute performance, but also to increase risk. That's right— improper diversification can actually increase risk. There is no need for rocket science, only common sense. We will take a practical approach to diversifying portfolios that will show you how to strip away a great deal of market volatility while actually enhancing overall returns.

Financial planning, and even investing in general, cannot be done in a vacuum. The world and the people in it are always changing. The dynamic nature of markets requires that we recognize the constancy of change if we are to reach our intended objectives. It is not difficult, but the requisite effort is more than many financial advisers wish to apply. By adopting the theory that markets are efficient, brokers and planners can build assets under management, allocate assets among a few asset classes, and go on about the business of bringing in new assets under management. As areas that were once inefficient become more efficient, new inefficiencies appear. There is always something new for the proactive investor or adviser. For advisers that subscribe to the passive form of management, the battle going forward is going to be uphill. Millions of investors now understand that markets don't behave in a manner we would always consider rational. Moreover, there is tremendous opportunity for profit in these market inefficiencies. Change can be intimidating, but investment advisers that embrace the inefficiencies of markets will find it empowering, and their clients will find it quite lucrative.

Our goal as long-term investors is essentially to improve both the proficiency and consistency of our returns. The first step is to understand the oxymoronic design of Wall Street. The theories espoused are predicated on a belief that investors cannot really do better than the general market over time, while simultaneously brokers spend hundreds of millions of dollars to convince you that their funds are most likely to outperform the market, while year after year the majority fail miserably. Wringing their hands, they twist and tweak their models, all the time failing to recognize that it is the rationale behind their models that holds them back. Meanwhile, there has been a quiet but very prosperous group of investors who are raking in amazing profits in markets going up, down, and sideways. In *Cashing in on Wall Street's Ten Greatest Myths* we tear apart the myths and uncover the core concepts that have consistently proved to safely build wealth.

1

Risk Is Diametrically Opposed to Reward

Many falsehoods begin as light permutations of truth. The sad fact is that despite overwhelming evidence to the contrary, many financial planners and brokers have en masse taught their client constituents that risk and reward are diametrically opposed. That is to say, they have taken two separate measures, the first being risk and the second being reward, and have given them equal weighting. Valuing risk and reward in this fashion makes the job of portfolio modeling easy, as the client simply identifies what degree of risk he or she is willing to accept, and voila—the probable rate of return sits beside it. Though this may sound overly simplistic, it is not far from what many individuals have been taught by their financial representatives.

So how complicated is the measure of proof that risk and reward are not diametrically opposed? Not very. When we assume that an incremental increase in desired outcome (a positive) carries with it an equal and opposite increase in risk (a negative), we are equating every investment decision with a play on a roulette table.

With this kind of reasoning, it is no wonder that many consider investing to be gambling. On a roulette table, a bet on a single number will carry a potential for two outcomes: One outcome is that the number will come up, and the money returns a multiple of the money gambled. The other outcome is that another number is hit, and the money bet is completely lost. In

1

the gambling scenario, the reward is inversely correlated to the risk. When investing in the markets, people also believe that reward is inversely correlated to risk. This, friends, is a myth. That's because the risk of investing can be mitigated or eliminated at any point by vigilant risk management.

GAMBLING

On a roulette wheel, there are 34 numbers. Numbers 1 to 32 are alternating red and black, and 0 and 00 are green. Simple statistics would tell me that on any given spin of the wheel there exists a 1-in-34 chance of achieving success. As this statistic is sometimes disheartening, players regularly choose to bet on a handful of numbers for a single spin to improve the odds. A player who bets on 17 different numbers on a single spin in theory improves his or her chance for winning to 1 in 2.

Active gambling enthusiasts are able to see beyond the spinning wheel and the free drinks to inquire about the payout. Most casinos will pay 32 to 1 for a single number being hit. Not bad when you're right. Since the wheel spins all day, every day, the house (the casino) is able to take advantage of the disparity between paying winners at 32 to 1 and the statistical payout where a player only wins on an average of once in every 34 spins. Simply put, a wheel that is spun 34,000 times will yield 1000 winners being paid 32 times their bet.

If all bets are made for a single dollar, the payout would be $32,000. The house would have earned $1 for each of the 33,000 losing bets (34,000 total—1000 winners) for a gross profit of $33,000 and a net profit of $1000 after paying out $32,000 to customers. Though there is still a variable that is uncontrollable for the house, the amount bet on each spin, the odds always remain in favor of the house.

So we can see that as a gambler, we have a defined reward for each measured risk we take. We also can see that there is no opportunity to change the measure of that risk or of its associated reward once the bet has been made (though I would be interested to hear of any success you have had in this effort in Monte Carlo or Las Vegas). Though risk and reward vary on the roulette table depending on the type of bet you place (i.e., red and black, which have much lower odds versus single-number bets, which carry much higher odds), the risk is still diametrically opposed to the reward. In fact, there is an inverse relationship. When you are right, you reap the reward of a nice multiple, and when you are wrong, you forfeit the entire amount that you bet.

INVESTING

Active traders and investors would interject here that in investing in equity markets (as an example) they do not expect to lose their entire investment; rather, they expect to use one of many stop-loss methods to moderate risk. As a result, an equity investor may invest $1000 and then put into place a stop loss that would automatically exit the position should the stock drop below a predetermined support level.

Depending on where the investor puts his or her stop, the loss would be limited accordingly. A loss limit of 10 percent would result in a $100 loss. Most investors and traders understand and appreciate this concept of *defining risk*, which is vastly different from the "defined risk" of a roulette table.

If we continue to extrapolate results from this and other examples, we gain an ever-increasing clarity.

> **EXAMPLE**: An investor feels there is an opportunity to double his or her money on a purchase of XYZ stock. The investor purchases 100 shares of XYZ at $50, with a total initial investment of $5000. Under the laws of probability, which dictate the theoretical outcomes on a roulette table, there is no allowance for (1) adjusting risk using loss limits or (2) reducing the size of the bet once the initial bet has been placed.
>
> The investor can, however, simultaneously establish a loss limit, whereby a drop in the valuation of XYZ stock would necessitate a sale of the stock, thus limiting the risk of any further capital loss. So if the 100 shares of XYZ purchased at $50 per share drop to $48 per share, the investor may choose to take a limited loss of $200. This is, of course, in contrast to betting the entire $5000 sum on red and the roulette wheel yielding a losing spin of black. On the roulette table the entire $5000 would be lost.
>
> Should the stock rise in price, the investor would have the opportunity to take profits "off the table" by selling the XYZ stock before it doubled in price, when it doubled, or even after it more than doubled, thus altering both the risk and the reward from its original model.

With very little exception, stocks tend to move toward an end rather than just arrive there. Stocks tend to trade at $49 and $48 and $47 before they reach zero. Are there people who hold stocks from $50 per share until they reach zero? Absolutely!

The psychology that creates this investor paradigm is one that we have spoken about in numerous seminars and is the subject of many wonderful books. Was it, and is it, necessary? Absolutely not!

An investor following a simple form of a *trailing stop loss* has an ability to monitor a trade or investment that is increasing in value while reducing and even eliminating a risk for loss as the trade moves forward in time.

TRAILING STOP LOSS: An order placed to lock in profits by selling a *long position* or covering a *short position* when the position changes direction in an unfavorable manner. Common trailing stop loss orders are given at a specific dollar amount or for a specific percentage retracement of the stock's most recent high (for long positions) or low (for short positions). An example is an investor purchasing stock XYZ at $50 per share and requesting a $1 trailing stop. If the stock goes to $55 over the next few weeks and then retraces down to $54, an order would automatically be initiated to sell the position. More common is the use of a percentage trailing stop. In this case, if the market price rises, the stop-loss price rises proportionately, but if the stock price falls, the stop-loss price doesn't change. This technique allows an investor to set a limit on the maximum possible loss without setting a limit on the maximum possible gain, and without requiring the investor to pay attention to the investment on an ongoing basis.

LONG POSITION, OR BUYING LONG: The phrase used to describe the purchase or ownership of a security. The act of "going long" can also be used interchangeably with the other terms to describe the purchase of a security.

SHORT POSITION, OR SELLING SHORT: The phrase used to describe the sale of a security that the seller does not own, or any sale that is completed by the delivery of a security borrowed by the seller. Short sellers assume that they will be able to buy the stock at a lower amount than the price at which they sold short. Stock to be used for selling short is borrowed from the broker-dealer. The broker-dealer has in turn borrowed stock from those owning the stock in their accounts. When there is no stock available to borrow, or when those who have loaned their stock wish to have it back, the broker-dealer is required to ask those who have sold the borrowed shares to replace them. Short sellers generally have to go back into the market to buy the shares back when this happens. Though this does happen, it is quite rare. Simply put, selling short is the opposite of going long. The short seller makes money if the security sold goes down in price.

The best gamblers in Las Vegas and Monte Carlo know that their initial bet is a cost of doing business; and in games like poker and blackjack, they can increase their bet when the numbers are working for them. Consequently, professional gamblers regularly pursue games where they can use an understanding of probability to increase the leverage of each dollar invested.

After many hands have been dealt with few face cards, a poker player may interpret a greater probability for face cards to be dealt given that face cards now make up a higher percentage of the remaining cards. This improves the likelihood for winning with what is already a competitive hand. Professional gamblers thrive in environments where they can maximize their dollars at risk. They commonly add to positions that have high-probability outcomes.

Once an increase in the bet is made, however, the poker player will either win or lose. Though the option to increase leverage through a hand of poker exists, there is no similar option for decreasing leverage. In poker, the only opportunity for managing risk is in folding (or exiting) a hand, wherein the entire bet is still lost. Risk going forward in the hand has been mitigated, but there is no protection for dollars already invested. So even in those games of risk where analytical skills can improve outcomes, each bet carries with it a measure of risk that is always equal to 100 percent. Conversely, an investor has almost complete control in efforts to reduce, mitigate, or eliminate risk at any time. Should an investor want to sell some or all of an investment at any time, that election exists. In fact, an investor can elect to go in the opposite direction. (We discuss shorting in Chapter 4.)

We may conclude from these analyses that in some forms of gambling (poker, blackjack, and other card games), the potential reward may be improved through leverage, while in other forms (roulette, dice, and sports betting), the risk remains inversely correlated to reward. The idea of this inverse correlation, however, is inappropriately used to color the financial markets.

As depicted in Exhibits 1-1 to 1-3, a world where reward is diametrically opposed to risk would provide finite results. A risk that holds a 30-to-1 payout when successful has a 1-in-30 for success (or slightly less in the case of casino odds). There is no in-between. In the stock market, an investor may use active risk management to reduce risk exposure while keeping the upside almost unlimited.

YOUR INTERPRETATION OF RISK DETERMINES YOUR PROFIT POTENTIAL

Remember Ben Franklin's aphorism, "A penny saved is a penny earned"? While this is true, a 50 percent gain does not compensate for a 50 percent loss. Nebraska-based Warren Buffett is considered one of the smartest investors in the country. He said he had become one of the wealthiest men in the world by strictly following two rules. One is not to lose money. The second rule is not to forget the first rule.

If our profession should be that of a ditchdigger, we strive to dig the biggest and best ditches for a person or company that offers the best pay. Is job satisfaction important? Without a doubt! Is it necessary? Absolutely not! If it were simply a matter of our gaining a sense of satisfaction or self-respect from our duties of employment, then we would continue to dig ditches even in times where no one was willing to pay for ditches being dug. It is difficult to seek those things that fill desires for achievement and self-esteem when more basic needs are not being met, as you can see in Exhibit 1-4, which presents Maslow's hierarchy of needs.

Though I know people who have done this sort of thing, I can assure you it did not last for long. Only those who have planned for this kind of event are able to work for long periods for free. The dollars they have saved allow them to serve in this way without any contingent income. For those who have not yet reached that point in life, there is little incentive; and in fact, there is great disincentive to work at any profession without compensation. We desire to put our skills and efforts into those things in which we get the most reward, whether as a volunteer or for income.

Why would anyone not expect the same from his or her investments? We may fundamentally like a company in which we are invested, just as we

Growth of $100,000 Account

YEAR	PERCENTAGE GAIN OR LOSS	ACCOUNT SIZE
1	20%	$120,000
2	20%	$144,000
3	20%	$172,800
4	20%	$207,360
5	−50%	$103,680
	Total return 3.68%	

EXHIBIT 1-1 As you can see, 20-percent-a-year returns can be quickly offset by one year of poor risk managment.

Growth of $100,000 Account

YEAR	PERCENTAGE GAIN OR LOSS	ACCOUNT SIZE
1	−50%	$50,000
2	20%	$60,000
3	20%	$72,000
4	20%	$86,400
5	20%	$103,680
	Total return 3.68%	

EXHIBIT 1-2 One bad year can take five great years just to return an account positive.

Growth of $100,000 Account

YEAR	PERCENTAGE GAIN OR LOSS	ACCOUNT SIZE
1	8%	$108,000
2	8%	$116,640
3	8%	$125,971
4	8%	$136,049
5	8%	$146,933
	Total return 46.93%	

EXHIBIT 1-3 Eliminating the sharp drawdowns makes all the difference in the world.

Maslow's Hierarchy of Needs

Self-Actualization
Personal growth and fulfillment

Esteem Needs
Achievement, status, responsibility, reputation

Belongingness and Love Needs
Family, affection, relationships, work group, etc.

Safety Needs
Protection, security, order, law, limits, stability, etc.

Biological and Physiological Needs
Basic life needs: air, food, drink, shelter, warmth, etc.

EXHIBIT 1-4 The Original Five-Stage Model. From Maslow, A. H. (1970). *Motivation and Personality* (2nd ed.). New York: Harper & Row.

may like our job, but what we *like* has very little to do with a guarantee of performance. Why would you quit a job that you enjoy and that pays you well? There is little reason.

On the contrary, why would you continue to dig ditches when payment for the work no longer exists? If your goal in digging ditches is to draw income, then working for nothing would obviously be ridiculous. So, then, why would any investor with a smidgeon of common sense find it logical to hold onto a stock or stocks that have failed to perform?

Worse yet, why would an investor listen to logic that requires one to continue holding assets that are plummeting in value? This is a distinction that should be clearly understood. In the work-versus-investment analogy, we noted that working without pay yields income somewhere in the neighborhood of zero dollars (much like a stock investment with no change in value and no dividend). Holding a stock that continues to drop in value is like digging ditches for a nonexistent employer while paying rent for the ditch-digging equipment. Not only is there no increase in wealth, but there is a marked decrease in wealth. I would challenge you to adopt these four rules for long-term investing:

1. Preserve capital.
2. Preserve capital.
3. Preserve capital.
4. Grow assets with consistency.

MEASURING RISK FOR MAXIMUM REWARD

In training professional investors and traders over the years, I have always stressed the importance of building both proficiency and consistency. At one particular seminar, a fellow remarked, "I am consistent—I lose about $200 every day." The room, of course, broke out in laughter, but the point was clear to all. Value should be given to being proficient as well as consistent. One without the other is not effective. The concept of consistent returns should be followed with an understanding that the returns sought should always be absolute in nature. That is to say, proficiency and consistency when combined should result in a smooth upward-trending *equity curve,* as you can see from Exhibit 1-5A. Note that the graph uses a measure called the Value-Added Monthly Index, or *VAMI.*

EQUITY CURVE: The equity curve is the value of an account graphed over a period of time. This curve reflects both the change in value of the account and the volatility of the account. Growth, positive or negative, can be seen by the net change as the account moves forward in time. The volatility is reflected in the up and down motion of the line as it moves forward. (See Exhibit 1-5B.) While volatility in the market may produce opportunity, volatility in a portfolio is always undesirable.

VAMI: The term *VAMI* is an acronym for value-added monthly index, which is a method for measuring the monthly performance of a hypothetical $1000 investment. The fluctuations in a chart showing the hypothetical performance are often referred to as a form of equity

Equity Curve Smooth

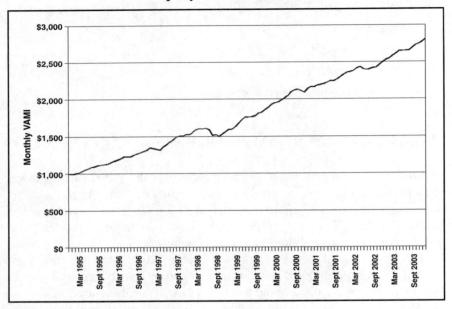

EXHIBIT 1-5A

Equity Curve Volatile

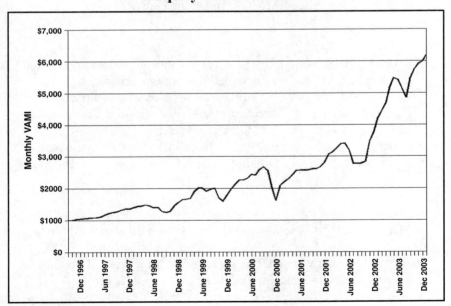

EXHIBIT 1-5B

curve. The value-added monthly index typically charts the total return gained by an investor from reinvestment of any dividends and additional interest gained through compounding. The VAMI is typically used to evaluate the performance of a fund manager.

The equity curve pictographically details the performance and volatility of a stock, bond, fund, or other security. The general trend of the line turning down (see Exhibit 1-6) should signal an investor to exit the investment. Historically, brokers have not defined specific rules for managing investments. Standards and even training focus on products to recommend to clients. The standard approach generally includes some mix of stocks, bonds, and mutual funds. Adjustments to the portfolio typically involve moving dollars from one asset class to another. Investors who have watched the veritable ruination of their retirement funds were not given a complete plan.

They were never given an exit strategy. Why? Because their brokers and financial advisers never had one and couldn't find anything else that was

Equity Curve Negative

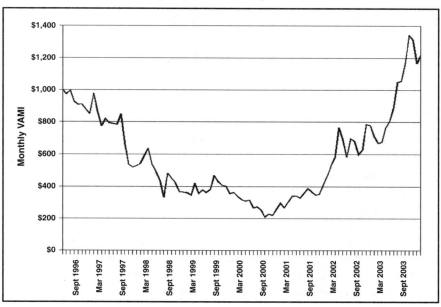

EXHIBIT 1-6

doing any better; and their mutual funds would charge large exit fees if they did not stay invested. So instead of stepping to the side, injury is added to insult with continuing losses. It must be the same logic used by the ditchdigger paying to rent ditch-digging equipment in the hopes that someone might eventually happen by who would like to buy one of the ditches being dug.

> *I been rich, and I been poor. Rich is better.*
> —SOPHIE TUCKER

Wealth is not like love. Where Tennyson mused, "'Tis better to have loved and lost than never to have loved at all," those who have tasted wealth and lost it are not always better off than they would have been had they never experienced the wealth at all. Oftentimes, they have become accustomed to a higher standard of living, including nicer homes, nicer automobiles, travel, and other luxuries, which can no longer be sustained when their portfolios have been devastated.

To educate investors on when they can improve their lot as a result of their investing versus when they must wait for the coming storm is a daunting task at best. Human nature is not well considered in the buy-and-hold model of investing, as we have witnessed now again.

MANAGING RISK FOR MAXIMUM REWARD

> *The future belongs to those who prepare for it.*
> —RALPH WALDO EMERSON

I just can't say enough about the importance of managing risk. All investors lose money at some time or another, but an investment should never be made before defining the risk and before deciding how that risk will be managed. The subject of risk management has never been particularly popular with the buy-and-hold (and forget) crowd.

The assumption that you must remain vested through thick and thin leaves very little room for risk management. So "forget" is precisely what buy-and-hold managers do. Growth and value funds of all ilks were forced to sell in 2000, 2001, and 2002 as the pain thresholds of buy-and-hold investors were sliced through like a hot knife through butter.

For years I have used the following simple exercise to drive home the importance of combining fundamental and technical analysis to manage risk: Suppose you have $100,000 invested in a particular stock or fund. If the fund loses 40 percent of its value or $40,000 over the course of a year, the value of the account is now $60,000 ($100,000 − $40,000 = $60,000). If the next year, the fund earns 40 percent, the account is now back to $84,000 [$60,000 + ($60,000 × 0.40) = $60,000 + $24,000 = $84,000], more than 16 percent and $16,000 below where the account began. Additionally, since the value of the assets is still well below their initial value, it will take another 19 percent return over the next year or two just to regain the last $16,000 lost in year 1.

For a young investor with 20 more years to recapture the loss, such an event will potentially be smoothed out over time. Parents who, during the time of loss or renewal, need to withdraw some of the funds for a child's education will find that the hole can grow exponentially wider and deeper. In this practical example, the power of *compounding* is lost; and where it is expected for long-term growth, actual results may not be sufficient.

COMPOUNDING: The ability of an asset to generate earnings that are then reinvested and generate their own earnings. At 15 percent interest for 25 years $10,000 would grow to $330,000.

THE RULE OF 72: In order to find the number of years required to double your money at a given interest rate or rate of return, you divide the expected compound return into 72. The result is the approximate number of years it will take for your investment to double. *Example*: If you want to know how long it will take to double your money at 8 percent interest, divide 8 into 72 and you get 9 years.

MARGIN AND VOLATILITY

Jeremy Siegel, a prolific writer and a professor at the Wharton School of the University of Pennsylvania, makes a recommendation that risk-taking investors with a 30-year investment horizon should seek a portfolio with an equity allocation of 131.5 percent. Siegel, like many others who have examined the opportunities for long-term asset growth, finds that equities are a key ingredient.

> *The way to wealth is as plain as the way to market.*
> —BENJAMIN FRANKLIN

Siegel, in no uncertain terms, recommends that astute investors use some measure of margin or credit to actually own more stock than they have in the underlying value of their portfolio. This is quite an endorsement for the aggressive use of stock investments in the portfolio structure. To appreciate both the risk and reward associated with this approach, it is important to understand *margin*.

MARGIN: Using money borrowed from a broker-dealer to purchase securities. An investor may borrow against assets in his or her account to buy additional securities, with the initial holdings serving as collateral for the purchase on borrowed dollars.

Margin is an incredibly effective tool for growing wealth. A note of caution, however, should be given to those who embrace the buy-and-forget mentality. The reason is that those investors who are no longer adding new funds to their retirement pool or are at or near retirement may exacerbate the toll a prolonged bear market may take on their portfolios. Added volatility may be acceptable earlier in the investment cycle, but it is much less desirable as we grow older. In a sample equity portfolio with 40 percent weighting in the S&P 500, 40 percent weighting in the NASDAQ, and 20 percent weighting in the Dow, a cash account beginning with a $100,000 balance would likely have seen assets grow to more than $600,000 before falling back under $250,000. If the same account were fully margined, assets would have rocketed to more than $1.1 million before losing two-thirds of its value and dropping back under $400,000 in value.

Many investors who bought new and bigger homes, cars, or borrowed funds for other investments based upon the a dramatic increase in net worth were shocked when perceived profits vanished. Exhibit 1-7 depicts the change in returns and volatility associated with the leveraged equity portion versus an unleveraged portion of the sample portfolio over the past 10 years.

Cash versus Margin 1993–2002

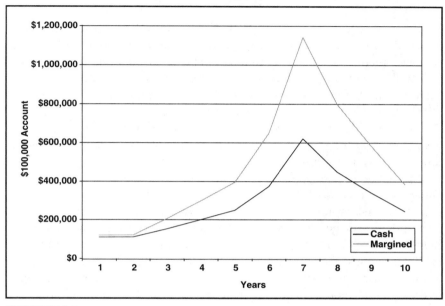

EXHIBIT 1-7

BUILDING RISK-AVERSE PORTFOLIOS
WITH STAGGERING RESULTS

There are numerous examples of traders and money managers who have mastered the ability to moderate risk while capturing tremendous returns. One of the most consistently profitable traders I know is Kevin Cuddie. As of this writing, Kevin has not had a losing month in his personal trading for more than three years. What seems more impressive is that his intramonth *drawdowns* (losses) have rarely exceeded 1 percent during a time when others were suffering massive losses (2001–2003).

DRAWDOWN: Reduction in account equity from a trade or series of trades.

RISK AND REWARD ARE NOT STATIC

If you tried to tell Kevin Cuddie that risk and reward are diametrically opposed, he would laugh out loud—and then he would ask what broker or financial planner sold you on that idea. Having been a regular guest on a nationally syndicated talk show, and being a respected trader and trainer, Cuddie says that he is frequently confronted with questions on what kind of return should be expected from a particular equity, sector, or fund.

We know that risk and reward are not static, but rather dynamic. Both the risk and the reward associated with a trade or investment change over time. If we were to purchase 100 shares of a stock at $5 per share ($500 total investment), we would have $5 per share risk should the company go under. Once that stock has risen in value to $50 per share ($5000 total value), the risk is now 10 times what it originally was, though the investment did not change. Some would say that by selling just enough shares (10 shares × $50 = $500) to recoup the initial investment, there is no "real risk." While this approach makes sense, we must never forget that the entire $5000 is now our asset and that we must modify our risk management accordingly. Even a simple modification in our plan will have tremendous long-term results in our investing. In this example, we can (a) sell enough shares to recoup the original investment and let the rest ride (sounds a lot like a gamble, doesn't it?), or (b) take some larger portion of our profits (say, $2500) and let the rest ride (still sounds a lot like gambling), or (c) take out our original investment of $500, reassess the fundamentals and technicals, and create a trailing stop loss that allows for continued growth while locking in profits should the investment change directions.

Due to his success as a trader, Kevin is always being asked what the next hot sector is going to be or what stock is ready to explode. His reply is always that the investor is asking only part of the question. To find out what the right questions are, we go to the interview:

RL: Kevin, what do you think is the dominating factor in your maintaining consistent profitability, especially in recent bear markets?

KC: Risk management! It is not a lot more complicated than that. I always maintain a good risk-reward ratio in any investment. Usually, it has to be a ratio of at least 2 to 1. If the risk is no longer outweighed by the probability for reward, I exit with no questions asked.

If risk is high, I will not establish any new positions. . . . If I am in a position and the risk becomes high, I get out. Of course, this means that I miss many trades that would have been big winners because I am very selective. But to me, missed money is better than lost money.

RL: There is a saying on Wall Street that suggests, "If you want to make more, you have to risk more!" What is your take on this assessment of risk and reward?

KC: The general public has been lied to. It's not true that to make big returns in business or investing that you must take great risks. There is always an associated risk with trading or investing or any business, but if it were not possible to reduce my comparative risk, I would have quit managing money many years ago.

Wall Street and the financial industry are no different than many other industries that have grown so quickly that they have failed to reassess their reasoning. Others are just afraid to think or try anything different than what the books have always said. I find it not only possible to increase returns with little risk, but I find it essential. You just have to have the confidence to ignore the old saying and old ways of Wall Street.

MORE PROFITS AND LESS RISK

Whether using a combination of fundamental and technical analysis, statistical arbitrage models, or one of countless other approaches to making money in the markets, the evidence against the old and cracked paradigms of risk and reward is overwhelming. Risk and its management are potentially the most relevant factors in the consideration of any manner of investment. Though risk does indeed impact performance over time, risk is not diametrically opposed to reward.

The profit can be incredible, with only a modicum of risk. Why then is it so difficult for mainstream money managers to perform well on a consistent basis? The myth that risk and reward are diametrically opposed is part of the problem. There are many more, including the flawed buy-and-hold strategy that is laid waste in the next chapter.

Managers and investors who have utilized a trend-following approach to trading indexes, and the equities that constitute these indexes, have proved time and time again the ability both to reduce the risk associated with swings in market volatility and to reap the rewards gained from proactive money management. We will cover more on trend following, market timing, and the prevarications of buy and hold in the next chapter.

Since the assumption by Wall Street has in large part been that higher returns necessitate equally high levels of risk, nothing more than this is offered as explanation or is considered appropriate. Mutual funds, hedge funds, and markets of all kinds have an ebb and flow. They fall into and out of favor for a variety of reasons. Many of the reasons are based in economics, while others are related to political influences. Even weather has an impact on the markets.

Generally speaking, there are three major directions the market can take: up, down, and sideways. There are three investment decisions to make in regard to market direction: be long, be short, and be flat. Each one is a separate investment decision.

When markets are trending upward, active managers may tend to be long. Downtrending markets will lead the same managers to be predominantly short. When markets are flat or sideways, so is the smart money because most of it's in cash. Remaining static is sometimes the most prudent investment decision to make. Taking no position in a stock is a position itself. It translates into preservation of capital.

Amazing profits can be yours once you recognize that risk and reward are not diametrically opposed. This change in thought will allow you to look at each investment in a light that gives you the upper hand. Everything, and I mean everything, you do carries risk. The risk comes in different shapes and forms, as does the potential for gain. Once you have established the criteria for measuring risk and for measuring gain, the next step is to evaluate the probability for each.

Some traders and investors have very low risk and very high reward, and though the probability for success in each investment maybe 5 or 10 percent, the rewards on the winners are gigantic. Investing in micro-cap companies is a perfect example. Oftentimes this stock group has low volume, which makes it more volatile. Moreover, the probability for success in each particular issue is difficult to measure. Stop losses regularly shake intrepid investors out of their positions, but the occasional high flyer can provide performance for the group that overshadows the many stagnant stocks. The key to profitable investing using one of these strategies is diversification and risk management. The more that assets are spread across strong prospects, the better; and the methods for limiting exposure and cultivating profits will determine the degree of success.

Other traders use high-probability trade scenarios where winning trades far outpace losing trades. Arbitrage is a perfect example of this type of approach. An arbitrage model may have a winning trade ratio of 90 percent or better, but the average loss may be a multiple of the average winner. In this instance, proper trade management may also suggest that the more trades done, the better, to reduce the statistical probability and potentially large negative impact of a single trade; but the early assessment of fundamental and technical analysis is much more accurate as a predictor of future results and can be used dependably before actually entering a trade.

Regardless of the approach, investors can improve performance by assessing and comparing the amount of risk per investment and the probability for success of that investment prior to investment. This mathematical or quantitative approach is rapidly gaining ground with mainstream managers, as it provides a metric for real statistical risk for a specific investment rather than the generalities that most firms conform to. Investors are now better able to know their potential for gain or loss over most time frames with statistical significance. We all sleep better as a result.

C H A P T E R

Benchmarking
Is the Best Measure

Historically, brokers and planners, trying to get clients to see the potential in equity markets, have used the S&P 500, the Dow, and the NASDAQ as evidence of the tremendous opportunity that exists by investing in U.S. equities. Exhibits 2-1 to 2-3 show the major market indexes over the past three decades.

30-Year S&P 500

EXHIBIT 2-1

30-Year DJIA

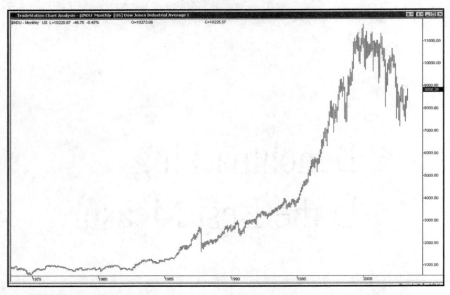

EXHIBIT 2-2

30-Year NASDAQ

EXHIBIT 2-3

These indexes are great indicators of how large groups of stocks move over time. Like an electrocardiogram (EKG), the rhythm and pulse of the markets is reflected in the charts of these indexes. As economic indicators, these indexes are wonderful, but the economy should not be the sole measure for what I, as an investor, expect from my investments.

A FALSE SENSE OF SECURITY

For years, some of the financial industry's biggest names have proudly advertised their performance in percentage points above a particular index. When measuring performance in this manner, it is referred to as a *relative return*. A source of never-ending irritation for those who know that risk and reward are not diametrically opposed is the constant comparison of performance to the market indexes, or benchmarking.

This guideline is a standardized measure of performance that has no practical value for the investor. I am at a complete loss for a reason why one would disclose such data. The only reason of any consequence would be that the presentation of performance in any other light would be less than impressive. This tendentious pursuit senselessly gives credit to the thought that simply beating the market is in and of itself a meritorious event.

Let's be honest. If you are planning to retire next year but the market has dropped 50 percent over the past two years like the S&P, or 36 percent like the Dow Jones Industrial Average, or 83 percent like the NASDAQ, do you really feel warm and tingly when your broker tells you have outperformed each of those markets and that you are only down 48 percent. Boy, if I could only lose that much every two years, just think of where I might be in ten years!

Even more grievous is the regular practice of investment houses paying bonuses to the managers of their mutual funds for performance above these benchmark indexes. So, while you have only lost 28 percent of your asset value in a fund, the manager is buying a new home in Aspen with his or her bonus because the fund still outperformed the indexes. Poor returns delivered under the guise of "outperforming the indexes" *should not* be acceptable to an investor who values *absolute return*.

ABSOLUTE RETURN: The goal of absolute returns focuses on the simple net return on investment as it is measured over any given period of time. This is in contrast to the goal of relative returns whereby the intention of management is the attempt to create a margin of outperformance against a benchmark. The benchmark is usually an index.

THE DISEASE OF RELATIVISM

Presently, benchmarking is standard fare served up by advisers and bantered about in the media by those who have little to no practical understanding of market utility or the goals of the average investor. Would it not make more sense to reward managers for their performance in comparison to managers of similar funds with a mandatory minimum percentage gain as a prerequisite for any bonus? This is all part of the disease of relativism in an institutional setting. It is nothing more than an institutional acquiescence to a side of humanity that never fails in transferring the focus of service to the provider rather than the recipient. Instead of setting standards low so that everyone might be involved, we should seek to keep the standards high so that the investing public is necessarily served by the best.

The sad result of this mind-set is its encroachment into corporate boardrooms, where senior executives are rewarded with incredible cash and incentives even when the company they are running is losing money hand over fist. When asked for justification for such enormous benefits packages, the standard answer goes something like this: "Mr. Johnson has positioned the company well for a recovery that will eventually put it ahead of the competition." Have you ever seen a farmer get paid in the spring simply because of the probability his seedlings could yield a profitable harvest in the fall? Hardly! As in the majority of businesses in a free-market society, he or she gets paid for *positive* results.

In the financial market, this focus on relative performance has birthed a nation of investors and investment advisers who are accepting of horrendous returns. They may be disappointed or discouraged, but many are still accepting. It is a paradigm that should be purged from the minds of the intelligent investor.

The idea that performance that exceeds that of the market for any period should be considered conclusive evidence of a fund's desirability is a myth. Wall Street has used this concept in the inculcation of unwary investors for decades. The fact is that *any* investing or trading strategy should incorporate an assessment of past and projected return as it relates to the volatility of the investment, the fundamental and technical evaluation criteria, and the standards for risk management.

THE BENEFITS OF ABSOLUTE RETURNS

The concept of absolute returns is empowering to investors who have felt for years like they knew where they wanted to go, and what results they desired, and which markets they were going to use, but had no exact idea of how the actual process should take place.

Rather than being at the mercy of the long-term trend of the stock market, where an investor has no control, the absolute-return investor is able to define expectations and set standards for each allocation of assets. Rather than sitting in the market waiting for it to do something, the absolute return investor actively moves assets to an area where his or her performance standards are being met. The results are synergistic. The opportunity cost of sitting in flat markets for extended periods of time is gone. The losses associated with sitting in poor investments during bear markets are negated. Most importantly, the psychology of the investor is improved since such markets and investments are actively engaged.

In coaching young children, we try to teach them that "getting suited up and coming out" is half the battle, and it is true (especially for children). Our goal is to have them participate and to gain a love for the game. But as they get older, we ask more of them. We want them to train harder, set goals, measure performance, and make the necessary changes to meet goals. College and professional coaches try to get players on their team that have a history of excellence, but they also understand that history does not win games—performance wins games. Players are pulled and replaced as needed. When all things are working, changes are few and far between, but good coaches are not hesitant to make changes when standards are not being met. Our goals may include retirement, a beach home, or any number of other things, but just "being in the market" is typically not one of them. Wall Street, on the contrary, is still intent on dressing us up in various funds and programs and having us watch as the market plays out.

My father bought me my first shares of stock when I was 13 years of age. He taught me to read the *Wall Street Journal* and to understand the basics of a balance sheet. In other words, he got me suited up and on the field. And it worked. I learned to love the markets and to appreciate the amazing opportunities that they offer. As I grew in my knowledge and experience, I began to expect more from my investments. In fact, I began to expect more from myself as an investor. The more actively I supervised my trades and adjusted my investments, the better I fared. I learned to focus on absolute returns at an early age, because I had no specific long-term goals as an investor. My goals were to earn enough to buy a new racing bike or to purchase a new car. Little thought was given to retirement. Interestingly enough, this mind-set of working diligently to get to the next milestone is easily adapted to reaching any financial goal. Even in my longer-term investments, I have been able to avoid significant loss by defining ahead of time expected performance parameters.

A focus on absolute returns rather than relative returns not only serves to modify one's desire for active risk management, but also creates a desire for new asset classes that meet more rigid standards. You will find over time as an absolute-return enthusiast that your portfolio has changed dramatically and that your comfort level has improved similarly.

Rather than being "dressed up" by your broker and forced to watch as the market unfolds along with your future, you can gain control of your financial future by demanding absolute and positive returns rather than whatever is dished out by the market.

MACRO TO MICRO

Kevin Cuddie, like hundreds of other great traders, is a master of what I call the "macro-to-micro" approach to investing and trading. Akin to the top-down approach, the *Macro to Micro* method begins by looking at the global economic picture in general but definable terms and then moving through a process of *fundamental* and *technical analyses*.

> **FUNDAMENTAL ANALYSIS:** A method of evaluating securities by attempting to measure the intrinsic value of a particular stock. Fundamental analysts study everything from the overall economy and industry conditions to the financial condition and management of companies.

> **TECHNICAL ANALYSIS:** A method of evaluating securities by relying on the assumption that market data, such as charts of price, volume, and open interest, can help predict future (usually short-term) market trends. Unlike fundamental analysis, the intrinsic value of the security is not considered. Technical analysts believe they can accurately predict the future price of a stock by looking at its historical prices and other trading variables. Technical analysis assumes that market psychology influences trading in a way that enables predicting

when a stock will rise or fall. For that reason, many technical analysts are also market timers, who believe that technical analysis can be applied just as easily to the market as a whole as to an individual stock.

THE VALUE OF TECHNICAL ANALYSIS

Much like medicine and investing, technical analysis ultimately involves the interfusion of art and science. From the analogy, you may already see the argument for technical analysis. Those casting aspersions on the use of technical analysis in investing always cite as proof of theory that technical analysis is not an exact science. Neither is medicine or rocket science; yet we continue to use medicine to help hundreds of millions of people around the globe each year, and we continue to send billions of dollars of equipment into space.

Why would so many pursue an inexact science? When trying to analyze the motivations of businesses, maybe we should "follow the money." The largest financial institutions in the world make decisions every day based on technical analysis. It works, and so they use it. Enough said.

Should we stop because the science is not perfect? The United States recently lost its second space shuttle, the *Challenger*, on reentry into the earth's atmosphere. The message that was shared by all the astronaut families who suffered in this tragedy was a desire for the space program to continue. These families, in a time when they were in unimaginable pain, were clear in sharing the passion their lost loved ones had for furthering the cause of space travel and exploration. The decades have brought invaluable insights into the way we approach space, and our knowledge only grows with the passing of time. We will find out what we did wrong, correct it, and do it right the next time.

Technical analysis is still growing, and like space exploration, it continues to improve over time. Technical analysis is here to stay, and the efforts to stifle its increasing popularity are growing more painstaking with each passing day. "The proof," as the saying goes, "is in the pudding." Technical analysis is used in some form or fashion every day by the largest financial institutions on the planet to manage risk and to earn profits. Literally hundreds of firms reap a significant portion of their profits from *quantitative analysis*, which uses both technical and fundamental data.

> **QUANTITATIVE ANALYSIS:** An analysis of a security that uses financial information derived from company annual reports and income statements to evaluate an investment decision. Some examples are financial ratios, cost of capital, asset valuation, and sales and earnings trends.

Exhibits 2-4 to 2-6 present simple examples of how a fund manager, using basic technical analysis, reduced volatility and improved profitability over a 12-month period. Could a human, made only of flesh and blood, actually use this methodology to maintain a favorable risk-reward ratio and still yield long-term results that are equal to or better than those obtained by just buying and holding? Absolutely!

S&P 500 Weekly with Crossover of Moving Averages, Reduced Volatility, and Increased Profitablity

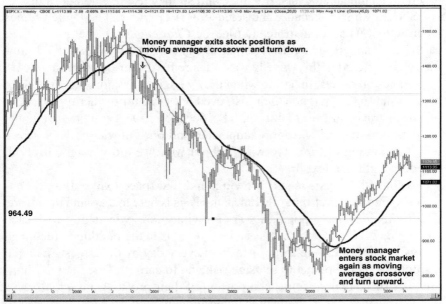

EXHIBIT 2-4

S&P 500 Daily with Crossover of Moving Averages

EXHIBIT 2-5

NASDAQ Daily: Benefit of Investing Both Long and Short

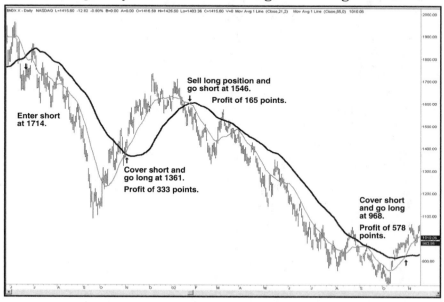

EXHIBIT 2-6

MAKING TECHNICAL ANALYSIS WORK FOR YOU

Investors and fund managers who use technical analysis find that the time frames utilized are most effective when they are dynamic. In other words, the points at which entries and exits are determined must be appropriate for the specific investment, as well as the time frame of the investor. These two are not always synchronized, and so they should be used as a filter for creating a portfolio that is functional for each investor.

Certain stocks, bonds, and funds may provide yield for a growth rate or dividend that is in line with the goals of the investor but carry too high an associated volatility, or they must be held for a time period too long for the investor's comfort. The end does not always justify the means. So the investor must find those particular stocks (or bonds and other investment vehicles) that will yield the desired results, with an acceptable volatility, over the designated time frame.

Someone looking to employ technical analysis to manage a portfolio of stocks intended to be core portfolio holdings will use longer-term charts like those shown in Exhibit 2-7.

CSCO Horizontal Support Daily

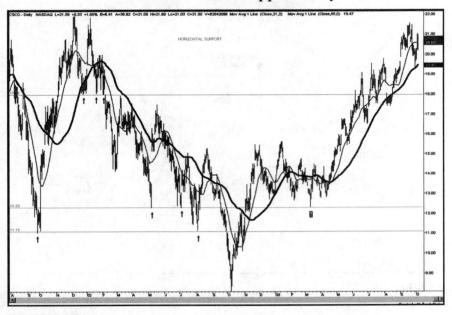

EXHIBIT 2-7A

CSCO Horizontal Resistance

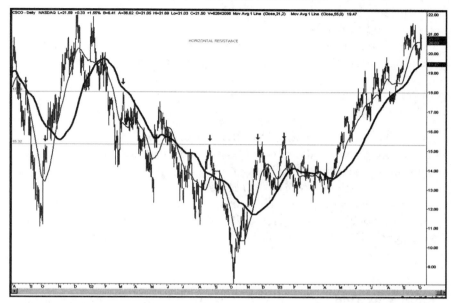

EXHIBIT 2-7B

CSCO Diagonal Support Resist

EXHIBIT 2-7C

Someone looking to employ technical analysis to manage a portfolio of stocks oriented toward more growth than value may look at a shorter time horizon. See Exhibit 2-8.

Would *dollar cost averaging* not offer similar results over time? It depends on what stocks are being averaged into and over what period of time.

DOLLAR COST AVERAGING (DCA): This investment strategy is designed to reduce the volatility associated with investing in equity and mutual fund markets through the purchase of a consistent dollar amount of a given security at regular intervals, regardless of what direction the market is moving. Thus, as prices of securities rise, fewer units are bought; and as prices fall, more units are bought. Dollar cost averaging (DCA) is also referred to as a *constant-dollar plan*.

Gold Max Reduced Vol and Increased Profits: Weekly Chart

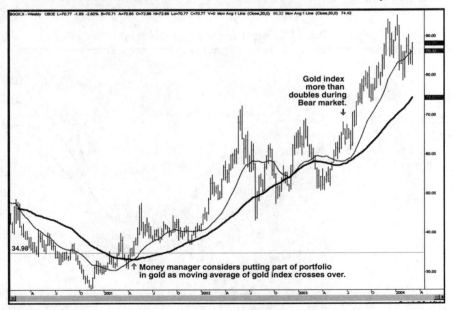

EXHIBIT 2-8

THE VALUE OF FUNDAMENTAL ANALYSIS
Below is a continuation of the interview with Kevin Cuddie begun in Chapter 1.

RL: What are your thoughts on fundamental analysis?

KC: Clearly, companies that improve their fundamental picture become more attractive "long" [buying with anticipation of an up move] candidates. The majority of Wall Street is focused more on fundamentals than any other element of the markets.

RL: Where does fundamental analysis have value?

KC: Through fundamental analysis, stocks with brighter than average prospects can be found. Without fundamental analysis, a trade is entered purely on the speculation of trends and price movement. Fundamental analysis in and of itself has merit, but when it is used alone, it is not only a flawed approach, but a dangerous one.

RL: Why is fundamental analysis, in your opinion, not enough?

KC: Fundamental analysis, when used alone, will often fight current price trends which can result in severe losses. Fundamental analysis alone ignores the masses. On Wall Street, the masses—right or wrong—move stock prices.

As we all know, the masses are not necessarily intelligent. They don't always act rationally. They will, however, break your bank if you don't listen to them, pay attention to them, and respect them.

Often, fundamental analysis will lead investors to buy when the masses are aggressively selling. Fundamental analysis may work long term—but at what cost? Should fundamentalists ignore price movement and market sentiment [technical analysis], then often they will be subjected to great losses.

The dilemma for the fundamentalists at that point, when losses are increasing, is how much pain do they take? Fundamentally, if nothing had changed, then the fundamentalists would hold on to their loser. Fundamental analysis will promote fighting the tape, holding losers, and averaging down—all strategies that are the trader's and investor's worst enemies.

RL: Is this the reason you would not use technical analysis alone to make an investment decision?

KC: Technical analysis alone measures only price actions, not reason. Big explosive sustainable moves require fundamental and technical factors to come together. For an explosive move to occur, all players in the market—the fundamental trader, the technical trader, the broker, the individual trader, the floor trader—must be on one side.

      They must all be thinking that a certain stock looks good in the same direction. That is what leads to the most explosive moves. Why ignore any factor that influences stock movement? Be patient and select stocks that have almost every factor leaning in the same direction.

      A note on the old fallacy [myth] that many technical traders believe in which says, "Technicals lead the news and fundamentals." For every time you can point to a stock that reacts positively before a good news event, I can show you one that sold off hard before a good news event.

      Another note to the technical trader—avoid excessively complex studies. Remember that all technical indicators and studies are in fact lagging indicators—based on price movement that has already occurred. The market moves on instinct and emotion. Don't get too complex with math to try to figure it out—as only chaos theory could come close.

RL: So you try to find ideas that have every controllable factor on your side while staying away from situations that have too many variables?

KC: If the fundamentals, recent corporate news, technicals, market action, sector strength, and volume are all pointing in one direction, what large player will take a large position against it? If every player is on your side—that is, when the risk-reward is heavily in your favor—then there is a high probability of success, low risk, and explosive upside potential.

      I am not saying that there is ever a trade where no one has a position against it, but there are many trades where most people are trying to establish a position on the same side as you—and that creates huge discrepancies between supply and demand—and that is where there is great reward with less risk.

FINDING GREAT PERFORMERS

As the case has been throughout the history of the world's major markets, the political structure and strength of nations and the associated macroeconomic cycles greatly impact the capital markets. Cuddie uses these macroeconomic measures to establish a baseline of influence for the domestic markets he trades.

The next step in the process of going macro to micro is to blend the news flow of key market participants and an understanding of how specific sectors rotate into a simple assessment of money flow. The news flow consists of government reports that measure the health of the economy, political changes that affect corporate governance and funding, and a variety of earnings and growth reports that impact investor opinion.

GOING MICRO

RL: Can you explain how you incorporate your technical and fundamental analysis into the macro-to-micro approach?

KC: Macro to micro is the filtering process I use to find setups where, most likely, every controllable factor will be in agreement with the position I'm taking, and there will be few, if any, factors left to chance. I always start macro, looking at the overall market, the big picture—because it's pointless to fight the masses. You must go with the flow . . . or as they say, "Don't fight the tape."

I then work to the micro. I look for sectors that are very strong or weak; it's not rocket science. If business is bad in a sector and the market is selling that sector, then there is no way I'll buy. . . . I will be looking to short [sell anticipating the stock will go down in price] bounces in that sector.

Going further micro—I will read every news development for as many stocks as I can, so that I can select the best candidate to trade within a sector. Perhaps retailers have had negative news, and the sector as a whole is selling off. By doing light fundamental research on each individual retailer, I can find the best candidates to short.

The effective use of this information is dependent upon a simple understanding of the companies that make up each *sector* and a comprehensive knowledge of *sector rotation*.

SECTOR: A sector is a distinct subset of a market, society, industry, or economy, the components of which share similar characteristics. Stocks are often grouped into different sectors depending upon the company's business. Standard & Poor's breaks the market into 11 sectors. Two of these sectors, utilities and consumer staples, are said to be defensive sectors, while the rest tend to be more cyclical in nature. The other nine sectors are: transportation, technology, health care, financial, energy, consumer cyclicals, basic materials, capital goods, and communications services. Other groups break up the market into different sector categorizations and sometimes break them down further into subsectors.

SECTOR ROTATION: Also called *rotation*, this term refers to the movement of money, by one investor or the overall market, from one or more sectors into one or more other sectors.

In the equity markets, sector rotation is the managed entry and exit of investment assets into different industry groups or segments as each group comes into or out of favor. Industry groups may be as broad as financial, health care, or Internet; or they may be much more specific, as in financial-brokerages, health care–HMOs, and Internet-infrastructure. Each broader category can be further broken down into more specific segments as illustrated in Exhibit 2-9.

Effective traders and managers using a macro-to-micro approach will often have a basic fundamental understanding of the leading industries and sectors before picking out specific stocks. In the continuing interview with Kevin Cuddie, we begin the final process.

KC: Finally, on the most specific level, I will run technical overlays to determine which of these final candidates have outstanding technical setups. It is those stocks in which I will take a position. The market, economy, sector, individual fundamentals, and technicals all bring me to the same conclusion—short! If all of the factors that I can research and control all say the same thing—I believe the trade is a good one.

RL: Kevin, this all makes complete sense, but how can the average investor make good use of this thought process?

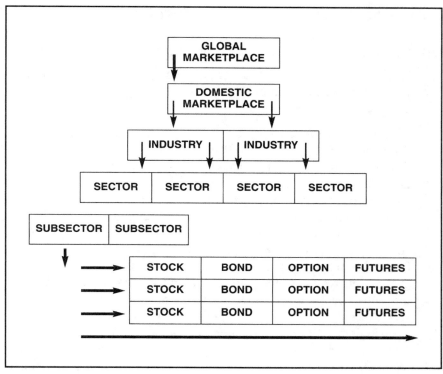

EXHIBIT 2-9

KC: Keep it simple. Perception, news, emotions, and reactions of the masses is what it is all about. Sit outside and calmly watch the masses react. It becomes almost humorous, and it is sadly predictable. I keep everything simple.

I don't crunch balance sheets and income statements. I don't run complex formulas for technical analysis. I just look at trends of price, trends of news events, trends in the broader market—and go with the flow.

I look for when the level of the stock is at a low-risk entry point! This is not just a system for finding trades, but also your system for risk control. If everything about a trade is perfect, except the risk is high—that's a bad trade. Risk is the trump card, and risk control is always number 1.

COMBINING TECHNICAL AND FUNDAMENTAL ANALYSIS

RL: Could you summarize your theory on the practical combination of Fundamental and Technical Analysis?

KC: Sure. Company fundamentals are what, over the long run, will have the greatest impact on a stock's price. However, the practice of using fundamental analysis alone is flawed.

Too many analysts focus solely on fundamental research and do not give proper attention to other risk factors that they should account for. Too many market risks, geopolitical factors, and technical factors drive stock prices and are too important to be ignored.

Sure, over 10 or 20 years they may be right in their analysis of the company's prospects, but can they weather the extreme turbulence and losses they may have to suffer through over those years? Fundamental analysis ignores recent price movements both of the stock and of the market. Subsequently, investors and analysts using only fundamental analysis will regularly buy or sell positions at very poor technical levels.

Fundamental changes in companies have a dramatic impact on long-term performance and will often move stock prices more than a technical change. This is due in part to the fact that fundamental changes have a longer-lasting and more powerful influence over stock price than technical patterns. This being said, I believe it is extremely important to find companies with improving fundamentals with a stock price level that technically carries little risk.

Buying and selling at prices at unfavorable levels can more than offset spectacular gains brought on by strong, fundamentally triggered price movements. Using technical analysis allows me to improve entry points on those stocks that were selected using fundamental analysis. This is critical in keeping risk in check, and the price improvement can lead to substantially improved results over time.

Many of the world's great portfolio managers prove year in and year out that a combination of technical analysis and basic fundamental analysis is essential in providing returns that consistently outperform the market while simultaneously limiting the risk and volatility normally associated with investing.

There are a multitude of reasons for uptrends and downtrends among the various market sectors. The effect of high-volume selling is often a steady decline in the price of the entire sector. When institutions decide there is more opportunity in telecommunications than in health sciences, they will sell health science holdings and purchase telecom. This form of institutional "sector rotation" is only one of a variety of causes of market fluctuation.

Many of these can be uncovered early by doing a thorough macro-to-micro analysis similar to the one we shared in Chapter 1. The problems really arise when buy-and-hold investors realize that the downtrends can be both extensive and prolonged. Matters worsen when we look at what really goes on in the mind of the investor and in the asset allocation models of real people.

SECTOR ROTATION

Those who have mastered an understanding of these fluctuations are ultimately able to identify the times when dollars are being moved from one sector to another by the major institutions. When this mastery is combined with simple technical analysis, risk can be kept at a minimum and potential reward can be maximized. Yes, risk can be less with one fund than another and yet outperform the market and the indexes (see Exhibit 2-10).

Sector Rotation Equity Curve (Conservative Model)

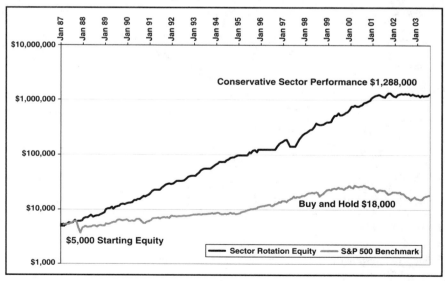

EXHIBIT 2-10

Exhibit 2-10 demonstrates the performance of a simple model we employ to rotate in and out of sectors with relatively few transactions per year. In some instances volatility is slightly higher, while in other instances volatility is slightly reduced. Even when you realize that the results are largely back-tested,* the results are still very dependable, as they are based on rotating in and out of mutual funds that have no price slippage. Exhibit 2-11 shows a similar model using a more aggressive approach. This approach also rotates among sector funds, but it is quite a bit more active; as you can see, it still outpaces the S&P 500 in 15 out of 16 years. Exhibit 2-12 gives the specific numbers for each of the strategies pictured in Exhibits 2-10 and 2-11.

There are a variety of similar models that only invest in sectors that are upward trending while moving some assets to cash when the general trend of the overall market is downward trending. For example, one model looks at all sectors that are fundamentally and technically bullish. Each sector is given a ranking, and then assets are divided among those sectors based on

Sector Rotation Equity Curve (Aggressive Model)

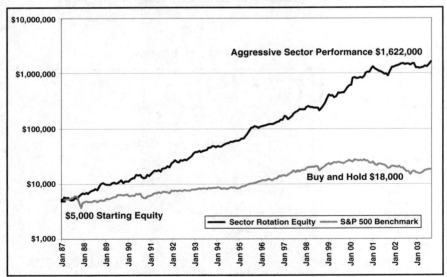

EXHIBIT 2-11

---

*Note: Back testing (or walk-forward testing as we call it when it is done properly) is still no guarantee of future results.

Sector Rotation Strategies

YEAR	S&P 500	Conservative	Aggressive
1987	2%	23%	37%
1988	12%	42%	45%
1989	27%	47%	13%
1990	-6%	44%	24%
1991	27%	55%	68%
1992	4%	42%	50%
1993	7%	61%	31%
1994	-2%	47%	33%
1995	34%	28%	77%
1996	20%	38%	36%
1997	31%	41%	54%
1998	27%	62%	51%
1999	31%	69%	75%
2000	-10%	63%	104%
2001	-13%	10%	6%
2002	-23%	2%	-2%
Average	**11%**	**42%**	**44%**

EXHIBIT 2-12

their combined fundamental and technical score. In this model all assets are invested long at all times. This may seem a bit aggressive in volatile markets or downward-trending markets, because allocations get heavily weighted into just a few sectors.

Another model, one that is perhaps more conservative, actually looks at both ends of the spectrum. This model ranks each sector based on the fundamental and technical ranking of each sector but then seeks to buy or go long the top five sectors while selling short the bottom five sectors. Using this methodology, investors may remain market neutral, meaning they are hedged against the general trend of the market and seeking to take advantage of disparate pricing between sectors. A popular area of investing now is the *equity market neutral* model.

EQUITY MARKET NEUTRAL: This strategy seeks to exploit differences in stock prices by being long and short in stocks within the same sector, industry, market capitalization, country, etc. This strategy creates a hedge against market factors. This is often considered the ultimate strategy for stock pickers and those who follow the volatilities of the stocks in each sector, because this strategy does best when the best stocks are taken as long positions and the weaker stocks are taken as short positions. For example, a hedge fund manager will go long in the 10 biotech stocks that should outperform and short the 10 biotech stocks that should underperform. What the general market does should matter less, because the growth in the group of better companies should exceed the growth in the group of weaker companies regardless of market direction. If the sector moves in one direction or the other, a gain on the long stock is offset by a loss on the short. In markets that are more volatile rather than steadily trending in one direction, profit is often made on both sides. The strong stocks can go up in price while the weak stocks in the same sector go down.

Analysis, both fundamental and technical, can be done on a daily basis, or specific criteria can be set whereby changes to the portfolio are made. In any case, the resultant decision making may be daily, weekly, monthly, or longer. Depending on the parameters used to build each sector matrix, the models may be anticipating the changes in each sector or following the changes in each sector. In reviewing a strategy, you should distinguish between the market-timing manager and the trend-following manager.

GET OFF THE BENCH

Those who are not familiar with technical analysis often group market timers and trend followers together when they are, in fact, quite different. Others have vilified both practices in praise of the buy-and-hold strategy that we know to be fundamentally flawed (no pun intended). The answer is simple. For investors to get the most from each investment dollar requires active management. Active management focused on achieving absolute returns requires more effort and more accountability. If you want your assets to achieve their greatest potential, your managers will have to, at least in part, incorporate some form of *market timing* or *trend following* into the mix.

MARKET TIMING: This strategy uses technical indicators or economic data to predict the future direction of the market. Mutual fund investors who regularly switch among fund asset classes to reflect changing opinions in their market outlook are also considered market timers.

Many academics believe it is impossible to time the market. Other investors, notably active traders, believe strongly in market timing. Floor traders, who work in the exchange pits around the world, make their living using market timing. What we can say with certainty is that it takes more of an effort to time markets than to buy and hold. Investors who do not have the time or resources to continually assess market indicators and make changes quickly and inexpensively are generally better off hiring a manager with the time and resources.

I skate to where the puck is going to be, not where
it has been. That makes all the difference.
—WAYNE GRETZKY

TREND FOLLOWING: Momentum investors often use the saying "The trend is your friend" to elucidate the concept of trend following. Another saying directed at active trades wanting to stay with the general flow of the market is "Don't fight the tape." This saying references the ticker tape that was the standard method for quoting stock prices more than a century ago. As the tape printed out recent transaction prices on stocks being traded, investors and traders were able to identify trends in the price movement of a security.

Those who consider themselves trend followers seek to reduce risk by maintaining investments that are in alignment with the general trend of the market. Additionally, they seek to capture profits more efficiently than others by identifying these changes using various forms of technical analysis.

Does this mean fund managers that adjust portfolios to reflect changes in market trends or employ market timing never lose money? Of course not! But, generally speaking, it does mean they will carry less risk and see less volatility and still yield superior returns over most time periods. This concept may seem simple, but it is vital to the search for the best investments and investment advisers. There is no reason for accepting what the market gives in the hopes that the best years will be those closest to retirement.

Whether they admit it or not, most brokers and even mutual fund managers make portfolio adjustments in response to the trends of the market. Managers are constantly switching from underperforming stocks to keep up with their peers who may be doing better. The reason they are switching has nothing to do with the fundamentals changing and everything to do with a change in market prices. The problem is changes are often made based on changes in stock prices without the use of technical analysis for guidance. Admittedly, the art and science of technical analysis can be somewhat complicated, but is it really so much to ask of someone watching over our life savings? Fundamental managers are always able to justify the purchase or sale of a security because fundamentals are so nebulous, but the funds they manage are valued on the market price of the securities held in the fund which forces them to be responsive to technical changes in the market even though they are not supposed to care. In fact, when their portfolios start to go south, they immediately look to sell losers and buy winners in the same sector. For years the practice of *window dressing* has run rampant on Wall Street.

WINDOW DRESSING: This strategy is used by mutual fund and portfolio managers near the year- or quarter-end to improve the appearance of the fund or portfolio before presenting it to clients or shareholders.

Performance reports and a list of the holdings in a mutual fund are usually sent to clients every quarter. The manager will sell stocks with large losses and purchase high-flying stocks to give the appearance that the manager had the best performers and stayed away from the big losers over the review period. This is not considered fraud, but it certainly raises moral and ethical questions.

Another variation of window dressing is investing in stocks that don't meet the style of the mutual fund. The manager goes to where he or she sees great opportunity and then realigns the portfolio before reporting. In this instance, clients really have no idea what they are paying for.

The bottom line is that window dressing may make a fund appear more attractive, and it may be a short-term solution for a manager whose fundamentals have not been supported by the market, but it cannot hide poor performance for long.

Window dressing is just one of the techniques used by Wall Street firms to make up for their lazy approach to the market. Infrastructure is supported by sales, commissions, fees, and banking functions that elicit tremendous revenue. Study after study has shown that very little can be directly attributed to the performance of the fund as compared with the market and the general allocation of funds into specific sectors. As much as 80 percent of portfolio performance can be directly linked to the allocation strategy. The same may be said for the equity portion of the portfolio, in that 80 percent of the performance may be drawn from the sectors represented. This may explain why sector funds tend to top the charts of best performers over most quarterly and annual time horizons. During any given period, two or three sectors always seem to dominate the field. This may also explain why sector-rotation models like the ones discussed earlier are gaining in popularity. Across the broad span of mutual funds the thought process of management is different. Instead of dependence on sector rotation or on good stock selection, most funds are largely dependent on the broad market going up.

After the recent market crash, billions of dollars exited their relative-return Wall Street firms in favor of absolute-return managers. This has triggered much of the old guard to modify its client offering to reflect absolute-return alternatives. Since the costs are thought to be much higher for this kind of offering, most firms are still limiting the effort to institutions and super-accredited investors. But you don't have to wait for them. There are choices if you know where to look. At a minimum, get an education in what to look for among fund managers and investing strategies. Firms like ETS Capital Management, LLC, where I serve as a managing member, regularly provide educational seminars for the investing public. Instead of waiting years for absolute-return managers to come to you through the normal channels, get off the bench and find the right one for you.

When deciding to whom you want to entrust your hard-earned assets, be sure to find an adviser who is an active manager, meaning he or she will actively seek out and find investments that are appropriate for you and the market environment. An active manager will help you to find investments that make money regardless of market direction.

Many active managers who consider themselves to be absolute-return advisers utilize both fundamental and technical analysis to manage assets under their direction. This is still no guarantee of making money every month or every quarter, but the path to building and maintaining your wealth should be far more pleasant.

MORE ABSOLUTE-RETURN STRATEGIES

There are numerous strategies that regularly demonstrate low to moderate risk while maintaining exceptional and consistent absolute returns. We have already looked at the macro-to-micro model used by Kevin Cuddie that has proved effective in bull, bear, and consolidating markets. There are literally dozens of similarly substantial models. One well-respected variety falls under the heading of *arbitrage*.

> **ARBITRAGE:** Arbitrage is an attempt to profit by exploiting price differences of identical or similar financial instruments, on different markets or in different forms or *different timings*. The ideal version is riskless arbitrage. The advantage is that it is often accomplished with minimal risk.

In the financial markets, arbitrage more literally refers to transactions designed to benefit from those opportunities or instances where inefficiencies or discrepancies exist in the pricing of a security or related securities. A practical example would be a difference in the price of a security trading in the United States versus the price of the same security trading in Europe or Asia. Should XYZ be trading at US$50.00 in U.S. markets and at the equivalent of US$50.50 in Hong Kong, an arbitrageur (one who practices arbitrage) might sell XYZ shares in Hong Kong while simultaneously buying equivalent amounts of XYZ in the U.S. markets. This sample trade would sometimes be done within the confines of a single trading session and would yield a return of $0.50 per share, or approximately 1percent. Historically, this type of transaction has proved to carry minimal risk.

There are concerns that generally confront this type of arbitrageur. Among these is the possibility of one side of the trade being broken after the fact by one of the other parties to the trade. Another threat to the arbitrageur is an inability to accurately determine how much is readily available to buy or sell on each side of the transaction. Sometimes another concern is just the simple inability to know when these opportunities are going to present themselves. Even with these concerns, it is plain to see that the reward is significant when compared with the risk taken.

Another form of arbitrage takes advantage of the disparities *between convertible bonds* and equities. Since convertible bonds are by definition convertible into the *underlying* stock, they normally trade at a premium to account for the seniority of the security and for the interest paid to bondholders.

CONVERTIBLE BONDS: A corporate bond, usually a junior debenture, that can be exchanged, at the option of the holder, for a specific number of shares of the company's preferred stock or common stock.

Convertibility affects the performance of the bond in certain ways. First and foremost, convertible bonds tend to have lower interest rates than nonconvertibles because they also accrue value as the price of the underlying stock rises. When the stock's price rises, the value of the convertible increases. In this way, convertible bonds offer some of the benefits of both stocks and bonds.

Convertibles earn interest even when the stock is trading down or sideways. Therefore, convertibles can offer protection against a decline in stock price. Because they are sold at a premium over the price of the stock, convertibles should be expected to earn that premium back in the first three or four years after purchase. In some cases, convertibles may be callable, at which point the yield will cease.

UNDERLYING: In an option contract, the security or commodity that is delivered when the contract is exercised. In securities, the common stock that is the basis of the company's other types of securities, such as stock options or preferred stock.

Take a 5 percent convertible bond maturing in one year at $1000, exchangeable into 100 shares of non-dividend-paying common stock currently trading at $10 per share. An arbitrage strategy might hedge against this long convertible bond with a short position of 50 shares of underlying common stock at $10 per share. Pricing inefficiencies between these two related securities, as we'll see, allow for profits both when the stock price rises and when it falls. A tremendous benefit to this strategy is the downside hedge. Gains are actually earned regardless of the direction of the bond price. This is due to the fact that convertible bonds can only fall in value to the extent that they reach their "investment value," which is just the value of the same company bond if it were not convertible. In this case, let's say the investment value is $930.

An investment position such as this would likely have the following return dynamics:

RETURN WHEN NO CHANGE IN STOCK PRICE

Interest payments on $1000 convertible bond (5%)	$50
Interest earned on $500 short sale proceeds (5%)	$25
Fees paid to lender of common stock (1.5% per annum)	($7.50)
Net cash flow	$67.50
Annual return	**6.75%**

RETURN WITH 25% RISE IN STOCK PRICE

Gain on convertible bond	$250
Loss on shorted stock (50 shares @ $2.50/share)	($125)
Interest from convertible bond	$50
Interest earned on short sale proceeds	$25
Fees paid to lender of common stock	($7.50)
Net trading gains and cash flow	$192.50
Annual return	**19.25%**

RETURN WITH 25% FALL IN STOCK PRICE

Loss on convertible bond (only falling as low as investment value)	($70)
Gain on shorted stock (50 shares @ $2.50/share)	$125
Interest from convertible bond	$50
Interest earned on short sale proceeds	$25
Fees paid to lender of common stock	($7.50)
Net cash flow	$122.50
Annual return	**12.25%**

As this example shows, if a convertible bond arbitrage position is properly constructed, it should profit not only from the bond coupons and short rebate but from changes *up or down* in the underlying equity price. In other words, if the stock price drops, the gain from the short common stock position should exceed the corresponding loss on the long convertible bond. Likewise, if the stock price rises, the gain on the long convertible position should be greater than the accompanying loss on the short common stock position.

The strategy really is as simple as it sounds, but being prepared is the key. Professional bond arbitrageurs must have all the pieces in place to make the strategy work. Should a brokerage firm charge a high execution fee or not pay the proper amount of interest on short positions, the profits can quickly be eaten away. That being said, professionals who have been doing this for years can provide very impressive returns year over year.

When the difference between the price of the underlying stock and the price of the bond widens or narrows to the extent that there is a clear disparity between the relative valuations of the two securities, an arbitrage opportunity presents itself. If the bond, for example, is overvalued relative to the underlying stock (even after considering all the factors that go into pricing), an arbitrageur may sell short the bond and buy the underlying stock in anticipation of either the bond falling in price or the underlying stock rising in price.

Examples of money being made with great consistency and little risk abound. All you must know is what to look for and where to look. Seek out investment advisers who are proactive in managing risk and have a logical strategy for making money in all markets.

Find managers that are consciously seeking absolute returns. The consistency of absolute-return based hedge funds over most time frames is evidence for an investment logic that values absolute returns rather than performance as it compares with a specific market index. We will discuss this more in detail in Chapter 6.

What makes absolute-return managers better than the rest? They focus on what is important: risk management and profit. They want the assets in their fund to grow as a result of performance rather than just from a good marketing department bringing in new investors. Performance is the primary goal of the absolute-return manager, not outperforming an index. The paradigm is different.

C H A P T E R

Buy and Hold
Always Works

I recently heard, on a nationally syndicated radio program, an advertisement by a representative of one of the nation's more prestigious brokerage firms touting its *"conservative* buy-and-hold strategy." This particular advertisement was given in a comforting tone and with a recommendation for investors to approach investing with patience.

WHERE THEORY WENT WRONG

Patience, in my humble opinion, should never replace prudence. The real irony is that this advertisement was in the summer of 2002, when this adviser had to be witness to the hundreds of thousands of individuals who could no longer retire or had to come out of retirement as a result of a bear market that began less than two years before. Almost as ironic is the Wall Street standard of sharing past performance of markets, indexes, and, of course, funds with the intent of suggesting future results (which is not in itself bad) while simultaneously spouting vituperative railings concerning the evils of "trend following." If the firms are not trying to establish comfort in the future from the past, or give a general prediction of the future from the past then what is the purpose of their advertisements? They are trying to derive a long-term trend from a previous trend. It can be shown in numbers, or as annual returns, or on a chart, but it is all the same. Data reflective of a series of related events over time when put together are used to create a "trend." For people who don't believe in trends, they sure do send out a lot of junk mail loaded with charts and statistics.

> *The Lady doth protest too much, methinks.*
> —SHAKESPEARE'S "HAMLET"

THE TWO FACES OF WALL STREET

Wall Street has two faces. One challenges the ability to better, much less predict, the broad markets. Reports are flowing off the presses regularly from the financial literati with data that show over the long run that no one outperforms the market. If this is the case, we need only to be invested in a handful of exchange-traded funds (ETFs) to get the same results that we can expect without the multiple layers of fees charged by most brokers and mutual fund companies. On the other hand, the same brokerage houses send out data showing how and why they are able to beat the markets over time. Something is amiss.

When investors are regularly calling in to the major financial television and radio programs to inquire about buying more of a stock that has dropped 80 percent for the purposes of averaging down in their long-term portfolio, it makes my stomach turn. I am not sure what is worse, the thought of millions of people losing billions of dollars in net worth because of their belief in a flawed theory or the thought of these same people not learning anything from such remarkably expensive lessons. The definition of insanity is "doing the same thing again and again, expecting a different outcome."

Have they not seen the devastation of such an ideology, or are they too ignorant to recognize the gaping holes in this investment model, or do they just not care? I certainly hope that the plea is ignorance. Moreover, I pray that light may invade this cave in which they dwell. The support for the "be patient, trust us, we invest only in the best companies" prattle in the advertisement discussed earlier was bolstered by market data revealing an annualized return of 10.5 percent over the past 75 years. I am sure that this and other well-meaning financial advisers have happily maintained these shallow thought processes for years—and apparently without ever questioning the veracity of their own rhetoric. It would appear that there exists a huge contingent of brokers and advisers that still do not see the error in their ways.

THERE ARE NO GUARANTEES

If the market were to go up and down within a very limited range for hundreds of years at a time, then the consequence of the buy-and-hold strategy would appear to be at the very least *less* tragic. The market, however, does not stay in such a tight range, which lends itself to risk that is not accounted for in a practical sense. In the now famous words of the 1992 presidential candidate, Ross Perot, "Let's go to the chart!"

The five-year chart of the NASDAQ (Exhibit 3-1) clearly depicts a tumultuous market period. But, there is a larger point to be made. This chart is unlabeled and each bar could easily be made to represent one hour, one day, or one year. The reality is that markets change. Global economies change. There is nothing mandating that any market will trend upward in the long run. The market is not bonded or insured. It is not backed by the full faith and credit of the U.S. government. In fact, there is not a mention in the scriptures of any major religion prescribing the securities markets as the proxy steward for our financial assets.

NDX No Guarantee

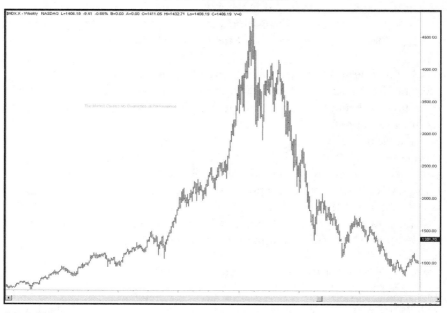

EXHIBIT 3-1

THE SUCCESSFUL INVESTOR PARADIGM

We as investors are accountable to ourselves for reaching our long-term goals. The global financial markets are one of the best *tools* we have for obtaining and securing financial independence. Before we put money into the market, we must set expectations and define consequences. By setting expectations we force ourselves to review the reasons for the investment, their appropriateness for our long-term goals, and targets for taking profits or adjusting our acceptable risk.

> **EXAMPLE:** The purchase of a low-priced stock that appears to be undervalued both fundamentally and technically is rewarded in a very short period of time by a tripling in the price of the stock. Though the fundamentals have not changed, the stock is certainly not "undervalued" anymore. The price-to-earnings (P/E) ratio is near the top of the range of other firms in the industry, and a chart of the stock's price reflects its rocketlike growth. The investor can choose (a) to sell the stock since it has already surpassed expectations, (b) to hold the stock since the fundamentals have not changed, or (c) to put in a trailing stop whereby the stock will continue to be held (allowing for additional upside) but will immediately be sold should the general direction of the stock price reverse.

In electing to employ choice c, the investor does not leave money on the table from a security that may continue to rise for whatever reason, but is assured of keeping a large percentage of the gains should the stock lose its upward momentum.[*]

Thankfully, if we maintain control of our investments by setting them on a course that defines their objectives and the consequences associated with meeting those objectives, as well as the consequences of failing to meet those objectives, we will be equipped for any market.

It is not just the tool, but how you use the tool, that is important; and it's not how your portfolio does compared with the market, but the net results of your investing, that matters in the end.

---

[*]Note: In the 1990s analysts continually altered previously accepted "norms" for fundamental analysis in an effort to accommodate for stocks trading at prices and valuations previously considered impossible. Some analysts found themselves justifying the purchase of stocks with P/E ratios of 1100 because other stocks in the same industry had P/Es of 1200. The absurdity could be considered an anomaly, a product of the era, but more are sure to come.

IDENTIFYING FALSE GODS

A key precept in the doctrine of "buy and hold" is that, over time, the market will always go up. Whether it is a chart of the last 50 years or of the past century, there is always a case to be made. But there seem to be few scapegoats for the financial lives of millions ruined in the last bear market (though I hear that there is strong support for the "If the market does not fit, you must acquit" defense). The gist of the message from Wall Street is that the market is a dependable source for long-term growth. As a tool for long-term growth, there is no argument, but to put faith in an institution just because it is a centerpiece for financial transactions is ludicrous.

Guided by the precepts of the buy-and-hold strategy investors are subject to the emotions of brokers, which predisposes investments to inconsistent decision making. Moreover, the investor will be subject to the lost opportunity cost arising out of the premature sale of stock. At first glance, this sounds contrary to the basic tenets of buy and hold, as it implies selling. But remember, the buy-and-hold broker is expected to keep you in companies that are fundamentally advantaged. Consequently, fundamentals when used alone remove almost all aspects of price action or trend. Another company, perhaps more attractive by balance sheet standards, may or may not see a significant change in price in the future. In the meantime, the price of the first stock may continue to rise. Opportunity is lost by exiting the investment too early due to fundamental changes. There is also an opportunity cost associated with being in a new investment that doesn't perform.

Worse are the consequences of holding too long. Fundamental figures like gross sales, margins, net profits, taxes, and write-offs are always *lagging indicators*.

> **LAGGING INDICATOR:** Any measure of price or performance that is derived from data that occurred in the past.

Lagging indicators give a snapshot of how things stood in the past. Dozens of companies in 2001 and 2002 showed few signs of fundamental distress while their share prices tanked. By the time the fundamentals were revealed, investors had lost billions.

Let's be honest: What happened over the past 50 or 100 years will never happen the same way again. The world changes, markets change—and then there's *the reality factor.*

In a world I like to call "reality," many people don't invest 10 percent of their income for 40 or 50 years without interruption. Many never invest that much, and many more never invest for that long before their anticipated retirement.

In this world of reality there are, also, life events, like marriage, death, divorce, children, illness, and job changes, that affect our investing habits. When these events are combined with the unpredictable nature of the markets, it is difficult to predict where we might end up. Here is a case in point. We will call our subject Bob.*

Bob has been working with a financial planner for more than a decade in preparation for retirement next year at the age of 65. If Bob's salary began at $2400 per year 40 years ago and has increased with the cost of living and merit raises at a combined rate of 10 percent per year, his salary in his last year would be approximately $98,750. If Bob regularly put 5 percent of his income into a company retirement plan (tax advantaged and invested in the S&P 500) and five percent of his income in the stock market (the S&P 500), Bob would have approximately $265,850 in combined assets at retirement without additional adjustments.

Scenario 1 depicted in Exhibit 3-2, shows Bob's contributions to his retirement and the total of both his tax-deferred account and his after-tax account. The return rates are based on the actual market performance of the S&P 500 over the same time period.

The second scenario, shown in Exhibit 3-3, assumes the same time period, 1962 to 2002, but with the addition of real-life influences on his savings. By some standards these life events may be all too real and maybe even too conservative. Others may feel Bob was not as diligent as most people in their investing discipline. In scenario 2 the combined assets available at retirement sum to approximately $198,500, which is about $67,350 less than in scenario 1. The impact that this 25% reduction has on retirement decisions is significant.

---

*Disclaimer: Bob is the name of person who is purely fictitious. This character has been created strictly for the purpose of demonstrating the practical effects of the Wall Street–endorsed fallacy we call "buy and hold." Any similarities between this character and any other person or place called or referred to as "Bob" whether real or implied is unintended, and quite frankly—irrelevant.

The financial impact from the life events that we all incur have a lasting effect that can be somewhat negative as we lose the benefit of compounding in the years to follow. Take a closer look at Exhibits 3-2 and 3-3, and a variety of things become evident. First the actual amount of gross dollars available on retirement in the more positive scenario 1 is not very exciting. For someone who has put 40 years into building a career with a salary of almost $100,000 per year, to have a nest egg that is not even three times as much could present issues. If Bob has paid off his primary residence, which he purchased 20 years ago, and he and his wife have no children left at home to support, his personal overhead should drop. However, there are plenty of other expenses to cover, such as automobile transportation, travel, entertainment, food, home insurance, home repair, life insurance, food, clothing, and health care, just to name a few.

Another notable point can be found in the twelfth year of scenario 2 (Exhibit 3-3) where the gross dollars invested actually surpassed the value of the retirement account due to a bear market. This means that Bob was putting money away for 12 whole years only to find that he was no further ahead by being in the market than by sticking his dough under a mattress. There are two notations about "reality" to be made in regard to this situation: First, Bob may have stopped investing altogether at this point after being greatly discouraged in the market. Consequently, he would have missed much of the potential gains in the market should it have moved up rapidly after that. Second, Bob may have started putting those savings in another investment, like real estate, where he may have seen tremendous gains in the decades that followed. He would likely tend to stay out of the market until he saw the market moving again, in which case he could potentially miss a significant portion of the gains again. In either case, many investors become disheartened when they see nothing to show for 12 years of regular investing, and as a result, they change their investing habits. Call it the human condition, call it greed, but basic psychology tells us that individuals like to see results. In the investing world the term we use for results is *returns* (absolute returns).

Another consideration not included in the scenarios is the issue of divorce. We don't like to talk about it, but it does occur in half of all marriages. When a couple or family goes through the process of divorce, there tends to be significant interruption to the investment process. Sometimes the asset base is split, which can result in the diversification of the portfolio being altered. In the recovery process, it is common for one or both parties to remove assets to purchase a new home or automobile. There is also

Bob's Retirement Plan

Year	Cost-of-Living and Merit Increases	GI	Pre-Tax Dep	After-Tax Dep
1963	10%	$2,400	$120.00	$96.00
1964	10%	$2,640	$132.00	$105.60
1965	10%	$2,904	$145.20	$116.16
1966	10%	$3,194	$159.72	$127.78
1967	10%	$3,514	$175.69	$140.55
1968	10%	$3,865	$193.26	$154.61
1969	10%	$4,252	$212.59	$170.07
1970	10%	$4,677	$233.85	$187.08
1971	10%	$5,145	$257.23	$205.78
1972	10%	$5,659	$282.95	$226.36
1973	10%	$6,225	$311.25	$249.00
1974	10%	$6,847	$342.37	$273.90
1975	10%	$7,532	$376.61	$301.29
1976	10%	$8,285	$414.27	$331.42
1977	10%	$9,114	$455.70	$364.56
1978	10%	$10,025	$501.27	$401.02
1979	10%	$11,028	$551.40	$441.12
1980	10%	$12,131	$606.54	$485.23
1981	10%	$13,344	$667.19	$533.75
1982	10%	$14,678	$733.91	$587.13
1983	10%	$16,146	$807.30	$645.84
1984	10%	$17,761	$888.03	$710.42
1985	10%	$19,537	$976.83	$781.47
1986	10%	$21,490	$1,074.52	$859.61
1987	10%	$23,639	$1,181.97	$945.57
1988	10%	$26,003	$1,300.16	$1,040.13
1989	10%	$28,604	$1,430.18	$1,144.14
1990	10%	$31,464	$1,573.20	$1,258.56
1991	10%	$34,610	$1,730.52	$1,384.42
1992	10%	$38,071	$1,903.57	$1,522.86
1993	10%	$41,879	$2,093.93	$1,675.14
1994	10%	$46,066	$2,303.32	$1,842.66
1995	10%	$50,673	$2,533.65	$2,026.92
1996	10%	$55,740	$2,787.02	$2,229.61
1997	10%	$61,314	$3,065.72	$2,452.58
1998	10%	$67,446	$3,372.29	$2,697.83
1999	10%	$74,190	$3,709.52	$2,967.62
2000	10%	$81,609	$4,080.47	$3,264.38
2001	10%	$89,770	$4,488.52	$3,590.82
2002	10%	$98,747	$4,937.37	$3,949.90

EXHIBIT 3-2

Total Invested	SPX Open	SPX Close	% Gain/Loss	Accrued Retirement
$216.00	63.1	75.02	18.89%	$256.80
$432.00	75.02	84.75	12.97%	$558.53
$669.60	84.75	92.43	9.06%	$894.19
$930.96	92.43	80.33	−13.09%	$1,026.99
$1,218.46	80.33	96.47	20.09%	$1,613.12
$1,534.70	96.47	103.8	7.60%	$2,109.99
$1,882.57	103.8	92.06	−11.31%	$2,210.72
$2,265.23	92.06	92.15	0.10%	$2,634.22
$2,686.15	92.15	102.09	10.79%	$3,431.32
$3,149.17	102.09	118.05	15.63%	$4,556.69
$3,658.48	118.05	97.55	−17.37%	$4,228.36
$4,218.73	97.55	68.53	−29.75%	$3,403.41
$4,835.01	68.53	90.19	31.61%	$5,371.27
$5,512.91	90.19	107.46	19.15%	$7,288.27
$6,258.60	107.46	95.1	−11.50%	$7,175.89
$7,078.86	95.1	96.11	1.06%	$8,163.97
$7,981.14	96.11	107.94	12.31%	$10,283.53
$8,973.66	107.94	136.75	26.69%	$14,411.45
$10,065.42	136.75	122.55	−10.38%	$13,991.22
$11,266.36	122.55	140.63	14.75%	$17,571.29
$12,587.40	140.63	164.92	17.27%	$22,310.39
$14,040.54	164.92	167.24	1.41%	$24,245.18
$15,638.99	167.24	211.27	26.33%	$32,849.52
$17,397.29	211.27	242.16	14.62%	$39,869.41
$19,331.42	242.16	247.08	2.03%	$42,850.21
$21,458.96	247.08	277.71	12.40%	$50,792.68
$23,799.26	277.71	353.39	27.25%	$67,910.29
$26,373.59	353.39	330.21	−6.56%	$66,101.84
$29,205.35	330.21	417.09	26.31%	$87,428.08
$32,320.28	417.09	435.7	4.46%	$94,908.31
$35,746.71	435.7	466.45	7.06%	$105,641.65
$39,515.78	466.45	459.27	−1.54%	$108,097.68
$43,661.76	459.27	615.93	34.11%	$151,086.72
$48,222.33	615.93	740.74	20.26%	$187,735.62
$53,238.97	740.74	970.43	31.01%	$253,178.44
$58,757.26	970.43	1229.83	26.73%	$328,546.80
$64,827.39	1229.83	1469.25	19.47%	$400,484.43
$71,504.53	1469.25	1320.5	−10.12%	$366,539.78
$78,849.38	1320.5	1148.08	−13.06%	$325,704.44
$86,928.72	1148.08	912.23	−20.54%	$265,856.56

Bob's Retirement Plan, Modified

Year	Cost-of-Living and Merit Increases	GI	Pre-Tax Dep	After-Tax Dep	Total Invested	SPX Open	SPX Close	% Gain/Loss
1963	10%	$2,400	$120.00	$96.00	$216.00	63.1	75.02	18.89%
1964	10%	$2,640	$132.00	$105.60	$432.00	75.02	84.75	12.97%
1965	10%	$2,904	$145.20	$116.16	$669.60	84.75	92.43	9.06%
1966	10%	$3,194	$159.72	$127.78	$930.96	92.43	80.33	−13.09%
1967	10%	$3,514	$175.69	$140.55	$1,218.46	80.33	96.47	20.09%
1968	10%	$3,865	$193.26	$154.61	$1,534.70	96.47	103.8	7.60%
1969	10%	$4,252	$212.59	$170.07	$1,882.57	103.8	92.06	−11.31%
1970	10%	$4,677	$233.85	$187.08	$2,265.23	92.06	92.15	0.10%
1971	10%	$5,145	$257.23	$205.78	$2,686.15	92.15	102.09	10.79%
1972	10%	$5,659	$282.95	$226.36	$3,149.17	102.09	118.05	15.63%
1973	10%	$6,225	$311.25	$249.00	$3,658.48	118.05	97.55	−17.37%
1974	10%	$6,847	$342.37	$273.90	$4,218.73	97.55	68.53	−29.75%
1975	10%	$7,532	$376.61	$301.29	$4,835.01	68.53	90.19	31.61%
1976	10%	$8,285	$414.27	$331.42	$5,512.91	90.19	107.46	19.15%
1977	10%	$9,114	$455.70	$364.56	$6,258.60	107.46	95.1	−11.50%
1978	10%	$10,025	$501.27	$401.02	$7,078.86	95.1	96.11	1.06%
1979	10%	$11,028	$551.40	$441.12	$7,981.14	96.11	107.94	12.31%
1980	10%	$12,131	$606.54	$485.23	$8,973.66	107.94	136.75	26.69%
1981	10%	$13,344	$667.19	$533.75	$10,065.42	136.75	122.55	−10.38%
1982	10%	$14,678	$733.91	$587.13	$11,266.36	122.55	140.63	14.75%
1983	10%	$16,146	$807.30	$645.84	$12,587.40	140.63	164.92	17.27%
1984	10%	$17,761	$888.03	$710.42	$14,040.54	164.92	167.24	1.41%
1985	10%	$19,537	$976.83	$781.47	$15,638.99	167.24	211.27	26.33%
1986	10%	$21,490	$1,074.52	$859.61	$17,397.29	211.27	242.16	14.62%
1987	10%	$23,639	$1,181.97	$0.00	$19,331.42	242.16	247.08	2.03%
1988	10%	$26,003	$1,300.16	$0.00	$20,513.39	247.08	277.71	12.40%
1989	10%	$28,604	$1,430.18	$1,144.14	$21,813.56	277.71	353.39	27.25%
1990	10%	$31,464	$1,573.20	$1,258.56	$24,387.88	353.39	330.21	−6.56%
1991	10%	$34,610	$1,730.52	$1,384.42	$27,219.64	330.21	417.09	26.31%
1992	10%	$38,071	$1,903.57	$1,522.86	$30,334.57	417.09	435.7	4.46%
1993	10%	$41,879	$2,093.93	$1,675.14	$33,761.00	435.7	466.45	7.06%
1994	10%	$46,066	$2,303.32	$1,842.66	$37,530.07	466.45	459.27	−1.54%
1995	10%	$50,673	$2,533.65	$2,026.92	$41,676.05	459.27	615.93	34.11%
1996	10%	$55,740	$2,787.02	$2,229.61	$46,236.63	615.93	740.74	20.26%
1997	10%	$61,314	$3,065.72	$2,452.58	$51,253.26	740.74	970.43	31.01%
1998	10%	$67,446	$3,372.29	$2,697.83	$56,771.56	970.43	1229.83	26.73%
1999	10%	$74,190	$3,709.52	$2,967.62	$62,841.68	1229.83	1469.25	19.47%
2000	10%	$81,609	$4,080.47	$3,264.38	$69,518.82	1469.25	1320.5	−10.12%
2001	10%	$89,770	$4,488.52	$3,590.82	$76,863.68	1320.5	1148.08	−13.06%
2002	10%	$98,747	$4,937.37	$3,949.90	$84,943.01	1148.08	912.23	−20.54%

EXHIBIT 3-3

Accrued Retirement	Events	Action	Monetary Reality
$256.80			
$558.53	Gets married	Planning family	Spending on travel
$894.19			
$1,026.99			
$1,613.12	1st child born	Buy new home	No extra investment
$2,109.99			
$2,210.72	2nd child born		No extra dollars
$2,634.22			
$3,431.32			
$4,556.69	1st in kindergarden	Extra expense	No extra dollars
$4,228.36			
$3,403.41	2nd in kindergarden	Extra expense	No extra dollars
$5,371.27			
$7,288.27	Begin grad work	Extra expense	New bills
$7,175.89	Wife begins work	Extra expense	Pays for school and
$8,163.97			some of grad school
$10,283.53			Pay toward grad school
$14,411.45			Save toward new home
$13,991.22			Save toward new home
$17,571.29	Purchase new home	Moving, furniture, etc.	Spend it all on new home
$22,310.39	Teen needs transportation	Buy new bike	Put off big expense
$24,245.18	Teen needs transportation	Buy used car	No extra dollars
$29,849.52	1st begins college	Borrow from retirement	Take $3000 from retirement × 4 yrs
$33,430.77	2nd needs transport	Gets a job/parent helps	Additional Insurance
$32,315.97	2nd begins college	Parent helps	Quit after-tax investing
$37,783.46			
$51,355.87	1st begins grad school	Sorry—get a loan!	Begin after-tax investing again
$50,633.28			
$67,889.66			
$74,498.11			
$83,790.98			
$86,583.35			
$122,233.72			
$133,035.94	Market doing great	Buy vacation home	Borrow 20K from retirement
$181,517.39			
$237,730.44			
$291,988.19			
$269,027.93			
$240,924.88			
$198,493.26	Retirement	Sell vacation home	
		Get second job	

an increased likelihood that one or both parties will cease retirement investing for a period of time.

Changes in family overhead are also not factored in, as they are completely unpredictable. Insurance costs have soared over the past three
decades to become one of the largest expenses in most family budgets and
by far the largest single expense among many retirees. Who could have
known what impetus this would have on a family's financial future 40 years
ago (or even 10 years ago)? Should the cost for education continue to soar,
people with young children today may resort to withdrawals from retirement plans to help fund college. The variety of unpredictable expenses is
innumerable.

One of the most basic and practical questions that arises out of the data
coming from the ivory towers is "Who is going to invest for 75 or 100 years
before retirement?"

In statistics the larger the samples number, the greater the confidence
interval or statistical significance. But the average return or annualized return
alone gives no representation of the kind of volatility that can occur or of the
specific risk for ruin in a leveraged portfolio. Someone starting an investment
in the middle of the 75-year window and retiring at the bottom of the curve
will fare much differently from the investor who happens to be born at the
right time, begins investing at the right time (near the bottom of the curve),
and retires while the markets are still tracking on the positive side of the curve.
This is important for a couple of reasons. Once we retire, we are no longer
adding funds to the pool that would otherwise improve the net results (dollar
cost averaging) should the market begin to move back up again. Instead we
are pulling funds from the pool. This creates opportunity for a second problem: If markets have a negative return, the decline in the pool is exacerbated
and the amount of time left until funds are gone is shortened.

The markets over the time frame depicted could not be considered atyp-
ical. If anything, they could be considered robust. There was, of course, a
dip in the major markets of the United States. The Dow Jones Industrial lost
38.7 percent from its high of 11,750 in January 2000 to its October 2002
low of 7197. Likewise, the NASDAQ Composite lost 78.4 percent from its
March 2000 high of 5132 to its October 2002 low of 1108, and the S&P
500 lost 50.5 percent from its March 2000 high of 1552 to its October 2002
low of 768.

To appreciate the impact of this change, let's go back to our example of
Bob, who had acquired more than $400,000 by early 2000 (see Exhibit 3-

2), yet holds assets worth less than $200,000 less than two years later (see Exhibit 3-3). This kind of disparity is to be expected when we invest passively and without performance standards for our portfolio. This may explain why many advisers today who learned on the passive art of buy, hold, and pray are now spending more time with puzzled looks of abandonment on their faces. Those not suffering the consternation continue to beat the buy-and-hold drum, refusing to change their tune.

But wait, there's more! As an investor using the buy-and-hold strategy, you need only to extend your retirement by a few years to regain the retirement equity that once was yours. After the crash of 1929, it was only 25 short years before the Dow was back to its precrash levels.

Here are some reasons you should not worry about your buy-and-hold portfolio:

1. People are living longer than ever before.

2. Many people enjoy the camaraderie of the workplace over family time.

3. Nearly 15 percent of those who retire say that it is overrated. (Don't ask about the other 85 percent).

4. If you continue to work and save during an extended market downturn, you could theoretically retire in only 15 additional years rather than 25.

5. The market rebounded after the crashes in 1973 and 1987 in only two years. This is almost a guarantee that crashes in the future will be shorter if they even occur at all.

This is not nearly as humorous to those who in 2001 and 2002 lost half or more of their life's savings. The numbers bear witness to a reality that is still too disturbing, too morose, for many to discuss. Additionally, many investors have understandably exited the market in fear (as they did in the 1930s, mid-1970s, and late 1980s) and will not take part in any substantial rallies that may obfuscate the long-term performance for brokers selling the buy-and-hold strategy. Sadly, a spoonful of sugar may not be adequate for this medicine to go down...perhaps a dose of common sense.

YOUR RIGHT TO RETIRE WEALTHY

In the U.S. Constitution, the American people declare their divinely gifted and inalienable rights. The American people have always valued freedom and liberty above all else. Every day citizens exercise their rights to speak freely, to worship freely, and to transact business freely. But when it comes to investing we have unknowingly given up our freedoms under the reins of a buy-and-hold strategy. What freedoms are these? Let me explain.

Financial markets today offer abundant opportunities for profit in markets that are moving up, down, and even sideways. Most market participants would agree that markets do not always go up. Yet we choose to focus our efforts on only this one-third of the markets by making investments that yield profits only when the markets are going up. This is evidenced by the overwhelming long bias of investment vehicles and strategies in the marketplace today. These products would not exist if the demand were not there.

BUY, HOLD, AND PRAY

In allowing money managers who pursue only one side of the market to control the majority of our assets, we as investors give up the freedom we are afforded to earn profits in all market environments. To suffer the natural up-and-down volatility of the market in hopes that the trend will, in time, continue upward is an unwarranted and risky assumption.

In addition to being subjected to great loss in an extensive bear market, the investor sacrifices the opportunity for profit in the same bear market. We are fortunate enough to have substantial means both for hedging our risk and for earning great profits in all markets. Many of the investment vehicles available today were not around a century ago. We should embrace our freedom to invest in these many opportunities for building wealth.

Financial markets around the world have evolved from goals shared by businesses and investors. When the European aristocracy funded ships for trade with the East in the fifteenth century, it was commonplace for the lords and merchants to share both the risk and the reward of each venture, as ships were prone to piracy and unfavorable weather. Most merchants had a ready and waiting market for imported goods and as such would generally prosper exceedingly if the ship returned and if the goods were intact, not spoiled, or dead, or infested. Okay, Okay, the risk was considerably broader than one might think.

To make the investment decision even more challenging, a merchant would often need to contract for those shares of the ship's stock months or years ahead of delivery. Ship captains often planned time lags to acquire products and to accommodate for trading along the way.

In support of the venture, merchants regularly provided much of the materials to be traded by the captain. Do you think certain Italian, English, or French merchants would have cherished the ability to sell their ownership in the stock on news of their ships sailing into hurricanes? Of course, many would have found great value in having reliable and immediate news available and in having liquid markets that would provide ready buyers when stockholders wanted to sell. Unfortunately, none of this was even remotely possible, forcing investors of the day into a classic buy-and-hold scenario.

The difference in these days gone by was that there was neither an efficient means to measure a stock's present value nor a liquid market in which to buy or sell an ownership interest. Reduction in a *risk for ruin* could only be had through diversification of investment dollars among assorted ships sailing at different times in various waters.

RISK FOR RUIN: The potential for loss over time that would result from aberrancies in market, trading errors, and more. The risk for ruin in its simplest form lets a trader or investor know the potential for total loss due to a specific strategy. In more detailed versions, the potential for differing levels of loss is calculated. For example two investment strategies that seem very similar may actually have differing risk parameters. One may have a 2 percent risk for ruin, while the other strategy would only have a 0.25 percent risk for ruin.

The fact is that had liquid markets been commonplace, shipowners and merchants everywhere would have actively engaged the markets to address their risk. With better risk controls, merchants of lesser means would undoubtedly have taken the opportunity to participate in the most exciting and profitable markets of the times. More investors would have logically sprung forth new fountains of funding, giving rise to more ship construction and the creation of new commerce.

Time passed more slowly in those days, though. So the global economic boom that began with Marco Polo in the late thirteenth century was profound but without the explosive nature of the Internet boom seen in the late twentieth century. This is likely due in part to both transportation and communication routes being very slow. Had market structures in that time been as accessible as they are today, it could certainly be theorized that more investors would have joined the markets, which would have resulted in even more ships being built and even more commerce being created during the same period.

The comparison of early commercial shipping to the Internet boom of the 1990s is not by accident. It is important to note that the concept and proliferation of free markets has generally been very positive, while the logic of simply buying and holding stock in the companies that take part in these free markets has proved to be far less rewarding.

Let's remember that the shipowners and merchants of old were essentially forced into a buy-and-hold strategy. When the expedition went smoothly and trades went well, all were rewarded handsomely for their time, effort, and risk. When trading went poorly along the way, or cargo was ruined in transit, or worse yet, the ship and its crew were lost to pirates or weather, the investment was a complete loss. The risk-to-reward ratio was extremely unfavorable.

Until the genesis of insurance for the shipping industry, the risk-to-reward ratio was similar to that seen in the casinos we discussed earlier. With the institution of risk sharing by insurance companies on the scene, large companies and investor groups were able to offset a portion of the risk in exchange for a payment of premium. When merchant ships paid these premiums, their collective risk was reduced by the insurers who shared in bearing the inherent risks. Profit margins were, of course, narrowed as a result of the added premium, but the levels of risk became tolerable enough that swarms of new investors came to the market.

The idea that risk could be well defined was enough to bring more investors to the market. You could say that this new confidence let "all ships rise with the tide." Once an investor knows and understands that there is an effective procedure in place to mitigate risk, he or she will naturally be more inclined to invest.

The greatest drawback in the buy-and-hold model is its failure *to address the management of the risk* that exists for every investor. Regrettably, this failure is a crack in the foundation of the futures of those who follow its precepts, and it has already led to the insurmountable ruination of uncountable millions of investors around the globe. Before sharing a brief quote, it is important to me that I proclaim my undying faith in capitalism, with all the fruit that it bears, both bitter and sweet.

More than 230 years ago, historian Alexander Tyler cautioned the founding fathers that the American experiment would eventually fail. He wrote:

> A democracy cannot exist as a permanent form of government. It can exist only until the voters discover that they can vote themselves largesse from the public treasury. From that moment on, the majority always votes for the candidates promising the most benefits from the public treasury, with the result that a democracy always collapses over loose fiscal policy followed by a dictatorship.

Tyler went on to note that "the average age of the world's great civilizations has been 200 years. These nations have progressed through the following sequence: from bondage to spiritual faith, from spiritual faith to great courage, from courage to liberty, from liberty to abundance, from abundance to selfishness, from selfishness to complacency, from conplacency to apathy, from apathy to dependency, from dependency back to bondage."

His words now seem like ominous foreshadowing as conscientious citizens grow more and more concerned with a government that continues to take more of its constituents' belongings for the purpose of redistributing them to its special interests. Those who recognize that the damage is not easily repaired are to be commended. Not everyone will listen, and not everyone who listens will follow. We can only hope and pray that enough will take action to save the rest.

In the financial markets, the misconceptions have already proved tragic. However, if we, as investors, will recognize the mistakes of the past and change our path, it will make all the difference in the world. Each investor must be accountable for his or her own success. If you want to take charge of your financial future, you must question the effectiveness of your plan. This means imagining as many possibilities for the future as you can and seeing if your investment strategy is prepared to do what you desire under each scenario.

Some things appear to be effective until they are tested. The buy-and-hold concept is one of those. When it comes to most things, I really like to keep it simple. In my effort to be the consummate handyman, I have finally settled on the maxim that you can fix most things with only two tools: WD-40 and duct tape. Things that don't move but are supposed to get WD-40, while things that move but are not supposed to get duct tape. I wish investing were as simple.

OPPORTUNITY ABOUNDS

Investors who do not question why the models that have become the standard for mutual fund management, portfolio design, and stock selection have not worked will continue to be victims. In free market societies, the opportunity to make money abounds. What the prudent investor must master is the method for capturing that opportunity without letting the spoils slip away. Even the largest of cattle farms use fences. They must be able to control their investment.

Over the several centuries that followed the boom of the import and export shipping trade, the market breadth grew in large part as a result of the same two drivers that affect most markets: fear and greed. People were greedy to reap the rewards of new markets, new products, and new lands. Their fear, however, was not of lost profits; rather, it was a fear of missed opportunity. In this context, fear can be considered absent as it is becomes consumed by the greed. Over the long run, this type of motivation generally proves to be unhealthy for the consumer and the market.

The same scenario took place in the 1990s but in an environment where many nations of the world were operating under free-market systems and were reaping the rewards of capitalism. This new appreciation for capital markets came with a surge in wealth among most economic classes. Not only were the thresholds for the middle class raised, but the number of families living at these elevated levels of prosperity grew with wild abandon as well. More individuals throughout the United States, Europe, the Far East, and Latin America entered the financial markets than at any other time in history. It seemed that all boats might indeed rise with the tide.

FRACTURED LOGIC

But when it came to investing, many people fell prey to the fractured logic of buy and hold. This mind-set produced investors with unwarranted confidence in the markets. Since markets should always move upward over time (under the buy-and-hold model), the investor that owns the most now should profit the most later.

Brokers and portfolio managers schooled in the ways of buy and hold rallied investors forward like pirates at an island picnic. They enthralled clients with wonderful companies bringing amazing products to market. This in itself is not an egregious act. After all, it makes complete sense to seek out companies that have great products and are well managed for investment.

Corporations that have innovative solutions to the world's issues and that have an experienced management team and growing sales and margin figures are certainly poised for success. If they hold distinct advantages over their competition, they are even more likely to succeed. An interest or following by analysts and institutions can help propel a company's stock upward too.

All these criteria are important in making a decision to purchase stock in a company. But there is little evidence to inform investors about when to *sell* stock in a company. All companies can't be successful, and all stocks can't go up. Common sense tells us that we must have a plan for managing this aspect of our portfolio.

Under the "buy" side of the common buy-and-hold myth, a secondary theorem would suggest that buying more during times that markets dip should serve to improve the investor's average price over the long run. Over years the practice of investing fixed amounts monthly (dollar cost averaging) tends to reduce the average cost per share (cost basis) over the long run. In a true bear market, however, specific attention must be given to each investment in order to determine risk and reward. There is no benefit to buying more stock in a company that is faltering. Pushing additional dollars into these issues is like adding fuel to a fire that is already eating away at long-term profits.

As an adult, I can remember only one time when someone said something so funny, so ridiculous, that I had to spit out my drink to prevent it from erupting from my nose. The occasion for this distasteful display was brought on by a caller to CNBC in 2001.

This caller was inquiring as about whether he should bring his cost basis down from the mid-70s per share by purchasing more of the stock now trading at around $2 per share! Spew! Chuckling, the CNBC host responded with something along the lines of (paraphrasing) "Though this would certainly bring down your basis in the stock, there may be a reason the stock has declined more than 90 percent." Do you think?

The sad thing is that the buy-and-hold strategy was so completely acceptable to the caller, he seemed to be truly astonished at the suggestion that he should consider selling his stock. Go ahead my friend—average in for those staggering gains.

There is nothing wrong with buying and holding stocks over long periods, and dollar cost averaging is generally a great way to reduce the average price per share over time and build a discipline for putting money away regularly. However, buying without a plan for controlling risk is, in my opinion, irresponsible.

Millions learned in 1987, and more recently at the turn of this century, that what goes up may also come down. Companies such as Enron, World-Com, and Kmart were considered best in class. Those who bought these stocks in 1998 and are still holding them have lost their entire investment. (See Exhibits 3-4 and 3-5.)

TO BUY AND TO HOLD

The absurdity of the buy-and-hold strategy can be found in the dissection of the phrase: buy and hold. Let's move on to the "hold" side of the equation. The assumption of the strategy is that once a good company is found, the stock is purchased and held. Since there is nothing associated with taking profits or limiting risk stated or implied in the phrase, it is simple to see that the gross amount of effort for this strategy is focused on the fundamental research and evaluation of companies. Only when better companies with better fundamentals come along is the first stock sold. There is no other exit plan. Where else in life's quests do we not have an exit plan?

Legendary investor Bernard Baruch said that there was only one question an investor should ask when evaluating whether or not to invest. He said that when you looked at a stock you already own, ask yourself every day, "Would I buy this stock today? If the answer is yes, then hold on or buy more. If the answer is no, then sell regardless of the price of the stock." Baruch became very wealthy following this simple rule. In other words, if the criteria that should exist to move an equity, option, fund, index, or commodity are not in agreement, then we no longer have an advantage in the marketplace, real or perceived.

We know that we can always get back into a stock if all of the moons get back into alignment, but when risk and reward are not in our favor, we go to another investment that is favorable. This concept is extremely valuable once you realize that even good companies don't always go up in price.

LOW VOLATILITY AND BIGGER PROFITS

Investing is no different from life's other great pursuits—timing is everything. There is a time to buy, hold, sell, or buy more if all moons are in

Enron: Stop Loss vs. 100% Loss

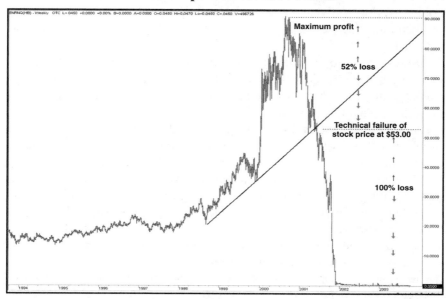

EXHIBIT 3-4

Xerox: Stop Loss vs. 75% Loss

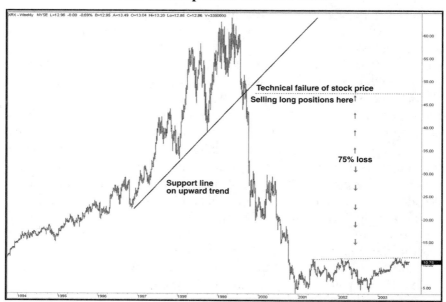

EXHIBIT 3-5

alignment, but don't just buy and hold and pray for the best. For buy and hold to work effectively, there must be a fair confidence that goals can be reached and lifestyle maintained even in the event of a poorly timed market crash.

Shrewd investors who understand the simple logic behind market timing have been rewarded over the past one-, two-, three-, five-, ten- and twenty-year periods with less volatility and more consistent profits in their portfolios. What is the opportunity cost of sleepless nights? I can assure you that those traders and investors using technical analysis and market timing to subordinate their long-term investing maintained a greater sense of peace and tranquility than their buy, hold, and forget acquaintances.

Traders on exchange floors are able to earn three, five, even ten times their account size per year due to the hyperactive approach they take to managing their money. Hundreds if not thousands of short-term traders are the same way. For every George Soros or Warren Buffett out there, I can show you a dozen traders who have made millions of dollars from their active trading style. This doesn't mean that you must make ten or twenty trades a day to see great returns. The difference is in the approach to the market. The passive investor depends on the market for his or her future, while the active investor continually analyzes investments to ensure they are appropriate for attaining goals.

Even if you feel that market timing is too dependent on anticipating market prices or direction, you can still enjoy the benefits of prudent risk management over the long run by *following* the broad market like some of the great money managers of our day. Take, for example, Paul Dietrich.

While Wall Street's minions have preached "When it comes to diversification, more is better," people like Paul Dietrich of Foxhall Capital Management (formerly Nye, Parnell & Emerson, Inc.) have been consistently building wealth for their clients. Before I share some of the nuggets from a recent interview with Paul Dietrich, I think it is important that you know a little about his background. Paul practiced international law for a number of years before entering the world of financial management more than two decades ago. His expertise in international business and relations gave him a solid footing for the launch of Meridian Emerging Markets, Ltd., a leading provider of information on global emerging market companies. Before entering the practice of law, Dietrich served as publisher and editor in chief of *Saturday Review*, one of the oldest cultural magazines in the United States. He also authored the award-winning book *A Guide to American*

Foreign Policy. Over the years he has made numerous contributions to the editorial pages of the *Wall Street Journal*, the *London Times,* and the *International Herald Tribune.* Presently Paul serves as the president of Eton Court Asset Management, Ltd., and the chief investment officer for Foxhall Capital Management, Inc.

Paul and I met through a mutual friend, Stephen Bolt, who founded Faith Financial Planners, a financial planning firm that has revolutionized the value-based investment world. We were both speaking at a conference on investing and had the opportunity to chat a bit. The discussion was enlightening to say the least. In my experience, managers who have been around for any real length of time tend to become part of the system, but Paul has maintained his views on making money undaunted by the ivory tower crowd. Let me share some of our discussion:

RL: Paul, you have been helping institutional clients since 1989, which means you have seen most every type of market there is to see.

PD: It has been an interesting journey.

RL: When you started out managing assets for a pension fund and a scholarship endowment fund, you must have been a little intimidated. That wasn't risk capital in those accounts. What were your thoughts?

PD: When I first started as a manager for these groups, their instructions were, "You can manage our money, but you can't lose any of our principal. And we don't want the funds invested in bonds and other fixed income—we want our money to grow, but—you can't lose any of our principal."

RL: We often say that our wealthiest clients are really concerned more about the return *of* their capital than the return *on* their capital. It seems to be a common dictum in the world of money management. What did you do?

PD: It took me awhile, but I eventually developed an investment discipline that took into account the desire for a strong risk management strategy by many of my most conservative clients.

RL: Did these clients expect to be in the stock market?

PD: Absolutely. Investors have come to realize that real wealth is primarily made in the stock market. But after the last bear market, everyone realizes the market can take it away just as fast.

RL: The market giveth and the market taketh away. How can you really control that?

PD: Our investment management objective is to reduce risk and maximize returns, with risk reduction and preservation of capital being the most important factor. Over the years I have tried to study the investing methodology and process of great and successful investors. They all seem to have one thing in common. They have surrendered to the reality of the market, the laws of supply and demand, and have learned to move with the market rather than against it.

Like a good football coach, they know that sometimes the market will give you the football and that you will need an offensive investment strategy to score touchdowns. Other times the market will, without warning, take the ball away, and you will need to immediately implement a defensive investment strategy if you don't want to lose the ground you gained when you last had control of the ball.

RL: So you actively switch teams or adjust your portfolio dynamically to changing markets?

PD: The bottom line is the market is always going to do whatever it's going to do, and arguing with it will always cost you money. When the stock market is broadly going up, we implement our offensive investment strategy, which is to heavily overweight your portfolio in stocks. But when the stock market is broadly going down, we will immediately implement our defensive investment strategy and move your investments to cash or bonds in order to protect your principal and prevent any substantial loss in your investment portfolio.

RL: In terms of broad market indexes, what does this mean for specific stocks and stock selection?

PD: A University of Chicago study by Benjamin King concluded that about 50 percent of the price movement (either up or down in price) of any security was caused by the direction of the overall stock market as a whole. About 30 percent of the price movement of a security was caused by the direction of the sector, and only 20 percent is caused by the underlying fundamentals of the actual company.

According to *Investor's Business Daily*, "when the general market—as defined by the S&P 500 index, the NASDAQ composite index, and the Dow Jones industrial average—tops and turns down, three out of four stocks, regardless of their quality or how they're performing, will go down."

Anyone who owned a stock between 2000 and early 2003 knows that almost all stocks and stock mutual funds declined because the whole stock market went down over that period. Even the stocks of well-known, great U.S. companies moved down during that bear market.

RL: So what specific tools or measures do you use to assess broad market direction?

PD: In order to determine whether we are playing offense or defense, I use two technical indicators. One is called the *S&P 500 Equal Dollar Weighted Index* (SPXEW), and the other is called the New York Stock Exchange Bullish Percent Index. These indexes track broad price movements in the market, and when they hit a specific level, we immediately implement the appropriate offensive or defensive investment strategy. We don't have to think or guess—we simply follow the direction the stock market is already moving toward.

S&P 500 EQUAL DOLLAR WEIGHTED INDEX: The S&P 500 Equal Dollar Weighted Index contains the same 500 stocks as the regular S&P 500 Index, but it assumes an equal dollar amount in each stock, bascially a set 0.20 percent for each of the 500 stocks. Whereas the better-known, captialization-weighted S&P 500 Index assumes the bigger the stock, the more percentage weight it carries in the index, this cap-weighted version is dominated by companies like General Electric, Microsoft, Exxon Mobil, Wal-Mart—the biggest stocks in the United States. The largest 20 companies (4 percent of the index) account for over 36 percent of the movement in the index.

RL: In essence, the S&P 500 is size neutral since it measures the performance of the 500 contingent stocks in equal weights. It gives more exposure to the smaller stocks in the index. Why do you not use the standard S&P 500 or NASDAQ 100 as broad market indicators? Are they not as intuitive?

PD: Precisely. There are a couple of reasons why I use the SPXEW. In addition to providing a soulless market indicator, I am comfortable enough in its robust nature to incorporate it as a discipline when combined with the proper analytics. Its robust nature comes from its structure. The Dow Jones Index and the regular S&P 500 Index tend to primarily represent the price movement of only the largest U.S. companies. The S&P 500 Equal Dollar Weighted Index tends to show market downturns and upturns before the major indexes.

RL: Why do you think this is?

PD: This is because large institutional investors like mutual funds, banks, insurance companies, and pension funds tend to sell smaller stocks before they sell their "core" holdings like GE or Wal-Mart in a market downturn. They also tend to buy smaller stocks first if they think the market is starting to move up. Since the S&P 500 Equal Dollar Weighted Index gives equal representation to smaller companies, this index tends to give an upturn or downturn signal before any of the major indexes.

RL: You mentioned the use of the proper analytics. Do you have a preference for charting these indexes?

PD: These indexes are best charted using a method called point and figure charting, which was developed in the late 1800s by Charles Dow. Charles Dow was the founder of the *Wall Street Journal* and the Dow Jones Industrial Average Index.

RL: Can you explain the basics of point and figure charting and what it does for you in the decision-making process?

PD: Point and figure charts are a way of recording stock prices that clearly depict the battle between supply and demand.

- You know you're playing offense when there are more buyers than there are sellers willing to sell. In other words there is more demand than supply—this always means the stock market is going up.

- You know you're playing defense when there are more sellers than there are buyers willing to buy. In other words there is more supply than demand—this always means the stock market is going down.

- When buying and selling are equal, prices will remain the same. In the end, the law of supply and demand is what moves stock prices.

RL: So, the first thing an investor must know is whether the offensive team or defensive team is on the field?

[Exhibit 3-6 presents a chart that graphs the price movement of the S&P 500 Equal Dollar Weighted Index.]

PD: Yes, exactly. When the chart is going up in a column of Xs, the stock market, as measured by this index, is going up. When the chart is going down in a column of Os the market is going down. Each X or O represents 30 price points going either up or down in the index.

RL: Paul, essentially you are identifying a trend and following it. For the investor that typically buys and holds, what difference would this make over time?

PD: Just as an example as of how well the discipline works in identifying whether the market is on offense or defense, look at Exhibit 3-7.

This exhibit shows how well an investor would have done using this discipline over the most recent recession and bear market from the end of 1999 to the end of 2003.

If you had started investing at the height of the stock market on December 31, 1999, and you just used the S&P 500 Equal Dollar Weighted Index shown in Exhibit 3-6 and (1) bought the index on the day it had moved up 90 points (3 Xs) from the previous column of Os and then you (2) sold on the day that the index moved down 90 points (3 Os) from the previous column of Xs, this would be the result:

- *39.25 percent gain.* If you only invested after the chart moved up 3 Xs and sold after the chart moved down 3 Os. The key is only changing strategy after the market has declared it's own broad direction.

- *20.43 percent gain.* If you just bought and held the S&P 500 Equal Dollar Weighted Index but didn't sell during the same period.

- *24.32 percent loss.* If you just bought and held the regular "cap-weighted" S&P 500 Index but didn't sell during the same period.

RL: This is completely counter to what Wall Street has taught investors for decades. In balanced portfolios, financial planners have always been taught to keep both teams on the field at all times. It certainly makes life easier for an investment manager if he or she doesn't have to make changes to a portfolio's structure every time the market changes direction.

S&P Equal Dollar Weighted Index (SPXEW)

```
1530   I - I - - - I - - - - - I - I - - - - - - - I - - - - - - - - - I - I - -          1530
1500   I - I - - - I - - - - - I - I - - - - - - - I - - - - - - - - - I - I - -          1500
1470   I - I - - - I - - - - - I - I - - - - - - - I - - - - - - - - - I - I - -          1470
1440   I - I - - - I - - - - - I - I - - - - - - - I - - - - - - - - - I - I - -   Top    1440
1410   I - I - - - I - - - - - I - I - - - - - - - I - - - - - - - - - I - X - -          1410
1380   I - I - - - I - - - - - I - I - - - - - - - I - - - - - - - - - I - 1 - -          1380
1350   I - I - - - I - - - - - I - I - - - • - - - I - - - - - - - - - I - X - -   Med    1350
1320   I - I - - - I - - - - - I - I - - - X - • - I - - - - - - - - - I - X - -          1320
1290   I - I - - - I - - - - - I - X - - - 5 - O - • - - - - - - - - - I - C - -          1290
1260   I - I - - - I - - - - - I - 1 - O - X - O - 3 - • - - - - - - - I - A - -          1260
1230   I - I - - - I - - - - - I - C - O - 4 - 7 - 1 - O - • - - - - - I - 9 - -   Bot    1230
1200   I - I - - - 7 - - - - - I - 8 - 3 - X - 8 - C - O - - - • - - - I - 8 - -          1200
1170   I - I - - - 5 - O - - - I - 5 - O - X - 9 - X - 6 - - - - - • - I - X - -          1170
1140   I - I - - - X - O - C - I - 4 - O - - - O - B - O - - - - - - - • - 6 - -          1140
1110   I - I - - - 4 - 8 - X - O - 3 - - - - - O - X - O - - - - - - - I - X - -          1110
1080   I - I - - - X - 9 - X - O - X - - - - - O - A - 7 - - - - - - - I - X - -          1080
1050   I - X - - - 1 - A - - - 2 - X - - - - - O - X - O - - - - - - - I - 5 - -          1050
1020   I - 3 - O - X - - - - - O - I - - - - - O - X - O - X - - - X - I - X - -          1020
 990   I - 2 - O - B - - - - - I - I - - - - - O - I - O - 8 - O - X - O - 4 - -           990
 960   I - A - 8 - A - - - - - I - I - - - - - I - O - X - O - B - O - X - -               960
 930   I - 8 - O - X - - - - - I - I - - - - - I - O - X - 9 - X - 2 - X - -               930
 900   I - X - O - X - - - - - I - I - - - - - I - O - - - O - X - O - X - -               900
 870   I - 7 - O - I - - - - - I - I - - - - - I - - - - A - X - 3 - • - -                870
 840   I - 6 - - - I - - - - - I - I - - - - - I - - - • - O - X - • - I - -              840
 810   I - 5 - - - I - - - - - I - I - - - - - I - - • - - - O - • - I - -               810
 780   I - 2 - - - I - - - - - I - I - - - - - • - - - - - • - - - I - -               780
 750   I - X - - - I - - - - - I - I - - - - • - - - - - - I - -                     750
 720   I - B - - - I - - - - - I - I - - - - • - - - - - - I - -                     720
 690   I - 4 - - - I - - - - - I - I - - - • - - - - - - - I - -                     690
 660   I - 2 - - - I - - - - - I - I - • - - - - - - - - - I - -                     660
 630   I - B - - - I - - - - • - I - I - - - - - - - - - - I - -                     630
 600   I - 7 - - - I - - - • - I - I - - - - - - - - - - - I - -                     600
 570   I - 6 - - - I - • - - - I - I - - - - - - - - - - - I - -                     570
 540   I - X - - - • - I - - - I - I - - - - - - - - - - - I - -                     540
 510   O - X - • - I - - - - - I - I - - - - - - - - - - - I - -                     510
 480   4 - • - - - I - - - - - I - I - - - - - - - - - - - I - -                     480
 450   • - I - - - I - - - - - I - I - - - - - - - - - - - I - -                     450
 420   I - I - - - I - - - - - I - I - - - - - - - I - - - - - - - - - I - I - -   420
 390   I - I - - - I - - - - - I - I - - - - - - - I - - - - - - - - - I - -              390
 360   I - I - - - I - - - - - I - I - - - - - - - I - - - - - - - - - I - -              360
 330   I - I - - - I - - - - - I - I - - - - - - - I - - - - - - - - - I - -              330
-----      I   I     I       I   I               I               I   I
-----      9 I 9 I 9   9 0 I   0   0 I 0           0 0 I 0
-----      7 I 8 I 9   9 0 I   1   1 I 2           2 3 I 4
```

EXHIBIT 3-6 *Source: Dorsey Wright & Associates*

PD: It is just not that easy. If your favorite football team only played with the offensive team on the field all the time, they would lose. They might do well when they had possession of the ball, but when the opposing team had the ball, your team would be scored on at will.

This is the problem most investors face. The hard truth is the market goes up and the market goes down. There is a time to play offense and a time to play defense. But if you don't know which team is on the field—you're going to have a problem.

Most investors only think one way. They just buy and hold stocks—always playing offense. Mutual funds are the same way. Mutual fund managers are paid to keep you fully invested in stocks at all times—even when the stock market is in a deep recession or bear market.

Four-Year Performance Using Point and Figure

Buy	Date	S&P EWI	Sell	Date	S&P EWI	Gain/ Loss
Buy	12/31/1999	1145.86	Sell	2/18/2000	1033.81	−9.78
Buy	3/16/2000	1112.80	Sell	3/14/2001	1182.86	6.3
Buy	4/18/2001	1244.06	Sell	7/6/2001	1225.20	−1.52
Buy	10/3/2001	1083.27	Sell	6/3/2002	1168.57	7.87
Buy	8/15/2002	996.23	Sell	9/19/2002	904.62	−9.2
Buy	10/15/2002	916.20	Sell	2/6/2003	925.94	1.06
Buy	3/20/2003	954.91	Sell	12/31/2003	1380.00	44.52

1	12/31/1999 to 12/31/2003 S&P EWI Investing only in Xs	39.25%
2	Above strategy after short-term capital gains taxes (40%)	23.55%
3	12/31/1999 to 12/31/2003 S&P EWI buy and hold (no switching)	20.43%
4	Above buy-and-hold strategy after long-term capital gains taxes (15%)	17.37%
5	12/31/1999 to 12/31/2003 S&P 500 Index buy and hold	−24.32%

EXHIBIT 3-7

RL: Once you know the direction of the market, how do you go from macro to micro in choosing the proper stocks to own?

PD: When specifically buying stocks, I have developed a discipline that has worked extremely well over the years. This strategy is fairly straightforward and is not "brain surgery." When selecting a stock, one has to ask two questions: what stock to buy and when is the right time to buy that stock.

1. *Sector outperformance.* I first identify those sectors that are outperforming the stock market as a whole.

   The S&P 500 Index is designed to represent the price movement of the entire stock market. This index holds 500 different companies in various industries grouped into 10 broad sectors of technology, energy, financials, consumer staples, etc.

   The actual S&P 500 Index performance is the "mean," and on any given day, some of these sectors are outperforming the S&P 500 Index and some are underperforming. History shows that sectors tend to outperform or underperform in cycles lasting for several months to several years. We all remember how the technology sector outperformed for almost three years in the late 1990s and then severely underperformed through most of the recent three-year bear market. My investment strategy is to only invest in those sectors that are outperforming the index.

2. *Stock outperformance.* Lastly, I try to select a diverse portfolio of fundamentally strong stocks with (1) increasing earnings, (2) good returns on equity, and (3) increasing cash flows that (4) are outperforming their industry peers and (5) are in a sector that is going up in price faster than the S&P 500 Index.

I am not sure why all investment managers don't use this strategy. Over the long run, it is not that hard to outperform the S&P 500 Index in the stock portion of your portfolio if you only invest in companies that have strong fundamentals; are outperforming their industry peers; and are in an S&P sector that is already outperforming the S&P 500 Index. As one sector starts to underperform, you sell stocks in that sector and buy stocks in the new sector that is rotating up. As I mentioned, it's not brain surgery.

RL: What about the resultant taxes on short-term gains from trading so actively?

PD: Good question. By using this discipline, you would have incurred short-term capital gains that are taxed at a higher rate than long-term capital gains. But assuming that you liquidated both portfolios on December 31, 2003, your after-tax total return was greater by 23.55 percent to 17.37 percent even though you paid higher short-term capital gains taxes to achieve the 23.55 percent after-tax return.

Many investors never develop a strategy to sell stocks because they don't want to pay the taxes on the gain. Unfortunately, they stick with a stock too long, and they end up not paying any taxes at all, because they no longer have a gain.

Over the years, I have always found that making the decision to buy or sell a stock based on tax considerations is almost always a serious mistake. Always make the buy-and-sell decisions based on the stock and market conditions first. Tax considerations should always be a distant second. It is better to pay whatever taxes you owe than to lose money and not have to pay any taxes.

RL: It seems to me that your approach might seem aggressive by some standards, including guidelines set down by government agencies that discourage a lot of activity within a portfolio, but it also appears that you would incur less volatility over time. Has this been your experience?

PD: It has. You know, there is an old investment adage, "Cut your losses quickly and let your winners run." Not following this advice is why so many investors lost money during the bear market of 2000 to early 2003. We review our stop-loss strategy weekly for all of the stocks we own in a client's portfolio. Buying a stock without knowing when or why you should sell it is like buying a car with no brakes.

RL: Eventually the road changes direction.

PD: There have to be controls. In the last bear market, industry leaders like GE went down by over 58 percent. In the pharmaceutical industry, leaders like Pfizer with earnings that improved 15 percent in 2002 over 2001 dropped 46 percent. When most companies weren't producing any earnings, they were, and they still suffered. Another drug giant, Merck, was down over 57 percent. Others fared just as badly.

Why did this happen? All of these companies had earnings during this period. No one believes people were using fewer drugs in 2002 than in 2001. There was no antipharmaceutical legislation in Congress. Why did all of these pharmaceutical companies drop by more than 50 percent in price? The answer is——nobody knows!

RL: This is a perfect example of how the broad market impacts all of the underlying sectors. But over time, can't investors depend on quality companies to bounce back?

PD: A recent *Investor's Business Daily* study concluded that "of all the best stocks of the last 50 years, the period of greatest market performance lasts on average only about a year and a half to two years. Some last up to three years. Only a tiny number of stocks have lasted for 5 or 10 years." Even the best stocks eventually go down. And when they do, they hurt you as much as or even more than the mediocre ones, especially if you buy them too late, as so many investors did as the late 1990s' bull market fizzled.

Nearly half of these market leaders never recover to their former peaks, and those that do take almost five years to do so. Remember this key historical fact: only one of every eight leaders in a bull market reasserts itself as a leader in the next or a future bull phase.

RL: So you consider your style of active management a more conservative model of investing than the old buy-and-hold model?

PD: Unquestionably, the investor who learns that it is better to preserve capital and lose opportunity than it is to lose money will find less volatility and better long-term performance than the buy-and-hold investor. Opportunity is easy to make up, while making back lost money is much more difficult.

RL: I couldn't have summed it up better myself.

In teaching interactive seminars and speaking at trading and investing forums around the country, I have talked with more than a thousand active investors in just the past five years; and many more during the previous decade. This is the feedback that I have gotten from people of all ages and with diverse backgrounds who have all been disappointed in the results of their buy-and-hold investment strategy.

My recommendation is to create a standard, or to find an asset manager that uses a standard, for limiting losses. This may include options, stop-loss orders, hedging, or more. The important thing is that you get it done to protect your assets. To keep it simple, remember the rule "If the reason you got in the trade is still there, stay in the trade. If the reason you got in trade is no longer there, then exit immediately."

This rule frequently raises additional questions. We will answer three important ones now.

1. *What should the reasons for getting in the trade be? Or better yet— how often can you really find a stock that has good management, has good earnings, is in an industry or sector favored by the institutions, is responding positively to the present global and domestic economy, has well-defined technical entry and exit points, and carries only a fraction of the risk relative to its potential return? (Most people don't ask it exactly that way, but you get the idea.)*

    ANSWER: Every day!

2. *How can an individual become adept at finding these opportunities?*

    ANSWER: The philosopher Epictetus said, "Only the educated are free." Learn as much as you can about the various markets and market sectors, the investment vehicles that are best suited for achieving specific investment objectives, and those strategies that seek absolute returns.

    Become a member of a local trading or investment group or an online community. Set aside time to learn from those who understand the values of both fundamental and technical analysis.

    You may also want to review the perspectives of some of the industry's great thinkers. Consider a reading schedule that includes the following authors and titles:

Milton Friedman and Rose Friedman, *Free to Choose* (Harcourt Brace Jovanovich, 1980); *Tyranny of the Status Quo* (Harcourt Brace Jovanovich, 1984)

Peter Bernstein, *Capital Ideas: The Improbable Origins of Modern Wall Street* (Free Press, 1992); *Against the Gods: The Remarkable Story of Risk* (Johnson & Wiley, 1998)

William J. O'Neil: *How to Make Money in Stocks: A Winning System in Good Times and Bad* (McGraw-Hill, 2002)

Mark Douglas: *The Disciplined Trader: Developing Winning Attitudes* (NY Institute of Finance, 1990)

3. What do I do when I have exited a trade?

ANSWER: Remember, being invested in a money-market fund is still being invested. Contrary to popular belief, it is not necessary to be in the market at all times to yield superlative returns. There is an opportunity cost associated with being invested in something through a cyclical downturn.

Money held in savings or money markets can earn interest while providing ready liquidity for new opportunities when they arise. You, as an investor, or your adviser under this scenario, are able to be selective about when and where you are in the market; limiting exposure to the markets to those times and places where reward clearly outweighs risk.

The repercussions from holding onto a loser cannot be measured just in the decline in the value of the asset. Interest that may have been earned over the period and profits from other investments that could have been made must be figured into the calculation to get a true measure of this opportunity cost. Holding an investment for months during a normal cyclical downturn is a waste of your two most valuable assets as an investor: time and money.

But what if it is a *really* good company? It doesn't matter! Quality, as much as we would like to objectify it, is still very subjective in nature. The corporate misdeeds that came to light during the market crash that began in 2000 are evidence of our inability as investors and analysts to accurately gauge a company's true value.

It is far simpler to assess a company's relative value and the market's perception of a company's value. It certainly would be nice if a simple fundamental analysis were enough to ensure investment success, but it is not. Many of those who put their faith into buy and hold during the 1990s, who also looked like geniuses, were later seen founding the Investor's First Church of Wishin', Hopin', and Prayin'.

Even with the support of investment magazines, investment newsletters, analysts' reports, and CNBC, most were eventually martyred. Their claims of long-term value were found unsubstantiated by investors around the world, including the lower middle class (formerly the upper middle class) and those now seeking additional employment to supplement their income (formerly the retired middle class).

I can only hope that the buy-and-hold horse that has been beaten upon repeatedly in this chapter is now dead. Sometimes that is all you can do. But just in case, we will include some intervention efforts for those who think that the "buy" in "buy and hold" serves to warn investors never to sell or short stock. Join us in the next chapter as we study the myth that the markets will always go up.

The Markets Will
Always Go Up

I can't tell you how many articles I have read written by experts and how many gurus I have heard speak on the dangers and evils of shorting stock. Just because the portfolios of these people have jumped off a bridge doesn't mean yours should do the same.

Before making a logical argument for including the shorting of stock as part of your investing repertoire, it may be prudent to give a brief description of the process. Essentially, shorting a stock is the opposite of buying a stock. If you buy a stock with an expectation that it will rise in price, then you sell a stock short with an expectation that it will fall in price. When you purchase a stock, you are considered to be *long* the stock and will see the profits from the investment when the stock is sold at a higher price. To short a stock, you sell stock that you do not own with the intention of buying the stock back later at a lower price.

SELLING SOMETHING YOU DON'T OWN

So how do you sell something you don't own? You borrow it from your brokerage firm. The brokerage firm uses its agreement with clients to borrow the stock that they own for the purpose of loaning it to others. This "hypothecation," or transfer, is never reflected in the client's account as it has been "loaned" behind the scenes and will be made immediately available if and when the original stockholder desires to sell. If, for any reason, the supply of the broker-dealer begins to run in short supply, the broker-dealer will go back to those who borrowed the stock (to sell short) to replace it. To replace the stock, the investor, now short, must go to the market and buy it back. The incidence of this sort of thing happening is extremely rare.

The trigger for a group of stock owners to corporately want to sell is generally a dramatic increase or decrease in the price of the stock. Big upward moves in the price of an equity drive some to take profits, whereas big downward moves in an equity's price bring in sellers trying to limit losses.

In more than two decades of trading, I have never personally been instructed to "cover" or buy back stock that I was short. In my oversight of hundreds of traders, I can remember only one incident. Since such an event is so rare, I will share the story. Additionally, you will see through this incident that even the exceptional cases do not come without adequate warning and that risk management is still a key to success regardless of your strategy.

In April 1998, during the height of the Internet frenzy, a well-known company in music sales and distribution announced a change in its marketing focus. Those of you who grew up as baby boomers will undoubtedly remember the name K-Tel. This record company built its success through consistent advertising and branding on television. One day, K-Tel decided that it would embrace the Internet and begin to push its products over the World Wide Web. This sounded like a rational decision. K-Tel was looking to keep up with the times before someone else entered what appeared to be a low barrier to entry into the marketplace.

One aside—K-Tel had not yet built a web site or brought about the functional support pieces at the time of the announcement. Likely the timing of the announcement was intended to let potential entrants into the space know that an industry leader would be coming in soon with all its marketing strength.

Needless to say, the announcement alone made the stock price begin to rise. In fact, on the day of the news release the stock closed up more than 50 percent at 6.125. An active retail trader in my office at the time began shorting the stock. Jake was surprised when the stock continued to rise the following day. So he shorted more KTEL. After all, the company was not even close to seeing any revenue from Internet sales, and it had the expense of building the web site and distribution system first. Jake was dollar-cost-averaging into the rising price of the stock in anticipation of its falling back to a "reasonable" price.

Economists often say that earnings drive stock prices. I would disagree, in that it is *the perception of future earnings* that drives stock prices (among other things). The "irrational exuberance" articulated by Fed chairman Alan Greenspan was clearly evident in KTEL. On the morning of the third day the brokerage firm notified all persons holding KTEL short (apparently there were a lot who thought like Jake) that they must replace the stock by market close. You can imagine what happened next. All those who were short had to go and buy the stock back. That made KTEL jump once more. Jake covered the stock as it opened at more than $12 per share (double the price at which he first began to short the stock) and as a result suffered a considerable loss.

I include this story to point out the importance of managing risk irrespective of your trading or investing style. There was no added danger inherent in Jake's being short. The reason for the magnitude of the loss was Jake's refusal to acknowledge simple rules of risk management, such as the use of *stop losses*.

STOP LOSS: A stop order for which the specified price is below the current market price and the order is to sell.

A positive note to this story is that Jake earned a large portion of his losses back the following day when KTEL broke back through key technical support and he shorted it again. Jake would be one of the first to tell you now that timing is everything.

This example is an extreme. Yet it did happen. There are dozens of fund managers who employ shorting regularly and have made tremendous returns in the recent bear markets.

You need not be one of the financial cognoscenti to see that markets go down as well as up. Markets have even moved sideways at times. Had Jake owned (been long) a stock that had bad news and continued to move down, he very well might have experienced similar results. Instead of people going to market to buy back their shorts, he would have seen sudden waves of additional selling as people incurring *margin calls* were forced to liquidate their positions.

MARGIN CALL: A call from a broker to a customer (called a *maintenance margin call*) or from a clearinghouse to a clearing member (called a *variation margin call*) demanding the deposit of cash or marginable securities to satisfy the Regulation T requirements and the house maintenance requirement for the purchasing or selling short securities or for covering an adverse price movement. Also called federal margin call or Reg. T call (for NASD requirements) or house call (for brokerage requirements).

Look at the companies listed in Exhibit 4-1. All these are now bankrupt. Buying more shares to reduce the average cost doesn't work when the stocks end up at zero.

THE CURRENCY MARKETS

Currency markets could not function without short sellers. Currencies are traded in pairs, like the USD/JPY (U.S. dollar/Japanese yen), the GBP/USD (Great Britain pound/ U.S. dollar), and the EUR/USD (Eurodollar/U.S. dollar). Each currency pair reflects an exchange rate between two currencies. In essence, when one *buys the USD/JPY "pair,"* one is *long* the U.S. dollar and *short* the Japanese Yen. If the same pair were *sold short*, the position held would be *short* the U.S. dollar and *long* the Japanese yen. The position taken (when we say we are buying the USD/JPY, we are long), whether long or short, in regard to the currency pair, refers to the first currency in the pair, or the one on the left-hand side. A currency trader *must take a short position* for every long position when trading a currency pair. The value of a currency in the global marketplace is most relevant when it is compared with another currency.

Selling short requires a specific state of mind. Instead of buying low and selling high, the objective for the short seller is to sell high and buy low. The objective is really the same; it is just accomplished in a different order.

Chapter 11 Stocks

Symbol	Bankrupt Firm	Business	High Valuation	Stock High
WBVN	Webvan Group	Online grocer	$1.2 billion	~$34
COVD	Covad Communications	High speed ISP		~$66
RTHM	Rhythms Net Connections	DSL provider		~$112
U	US Airways	Airline		~$83
TSIX	360 Networks	Fiber optic commun.		
KOOP	Dr. Koop.com	Internet health site		~$46
EGGS	Egghead.com	Internet tech marketer		
CPTH	Critical Path	Hosted messaging		
ENRN	Enron	Energy market		
ETYS	eToys	Internet toy sales	~$10 billion	~$86
ATHM	Excite at Home	Global media		~$106+
EXDS	Exodus Communications	Internet infrastructure		~$90
GX	Global Crossing	Intl. fiber optics		~$54
GSTRF	Globalstar	Satellite telecom		
GBFE	Golden Books	Children's books		
HOMS	Homestore.com	Online real estate media		~$138
ICGC	ICG Communications	Telecom	$2 billion	~$33
IRID	Iridium	Satellite telecom		~$70
KMT	Kmart	Discount retailer		
MCLD	McLeod USA	Telecom		
PRGN	Peregrine Systems			$80
PETS	Pets.com	Online pet supplies		
PHL	Planet Hollywood Intl	Restaurant chain		
	Polaroid	Photographic supplies		
PSIN	PSI Net			
VUSA	Value America			$56
WCG	Williams Communications	National fiber optic		
WCII	Winstar Communications	Telecom		
WCOM	WorldCom	Global telecom		
TGLO	theglobe.com	Interactive entertainment		~$97
XOXO	XO Communication	Broadband provider		

EXHIBIT 4-1

If we break it down to its simplest form, we invest for returns that we expect to be better than those we might earn from not investing. In purchasing a stock, we seek to earn a return, through dividends or through an increase in the stock price, that exceeds what we might expect by leaving the same funds in a savings account or money-market fund. Consequently, prudent risk management would lead us to sell a stock and put the funds back into the bank if our expectations no longer held. Short selling is the next simple step in the process. If we think that the change in price would yield a significantly greater return than what would be earned in the bank, we should pursue that possibility.

WHY SHORTING IS MISUNDERSTOOD

Short sellers are not always the most popular people on Wall Street. Many investors, broker-dealers, and investment banking firms see short selling as "un-American" and "betting against the home team." Some even go so far as to suggest that short sellers are a primary cause of major market downturns, like the crash of 1987.

What about the negative impact shorting can have on a company? When people that own stock are selling their interest and short sellers enter the market concurrently, the stock price tends to fall. Great! In capitalist markets positive perceptions are rewarded just as negative perceptions are punished. If you add up all the times a public company has been shorted out of existence, you would come up with a grand total of...zero! Companies fail because their business model fails, because their cash flows are negative, because of poor management, but *not* because of heavy short selling.

Market regulations in most U.S.-based markets attempt to make the shorting of stock undesirable through the institution of rules like the SEC short sale rule (which requires short sales to be made only on a plus tick or zero plus tick). Essentially, this rule means that short sales can only be made in a rising market. This rule is designed to prevent raiders from selling short to drive a stock down. This rule, also called the plus-tick rule or tick-test rule, was instituted by regulators in answer to unfounded charges that short sellers were a major cause of market downturns. There is still no data showing short selling to have a negative impact on markets, but the rule still stands.

To the contrary, short selling plays an important role in the marketplace. It provides liquidity, drives down overpriced securities, and generally increases the efficiencies of the markets. In fact, some of the greatest research is done by short sellers looking for important signs that mark a company losing its edge. Where potential conflicts of interest from investment-banking firms are a concern for purchases of analyst-recommended stocks, those recommended short sales tend to be free of such uneasiness. Consequently, short sellers provide not only a first line of defense against financial malfeasance, but also a voice of reason in overly optimistic markets. This unbiased introspection may actually be responsible for the prevention of market crashes as short sellers introduce a measure of common sense to markets raging with emotion.

To sell a stock short, you must find a party willing to buy the stock at your selling price. This party, for whatever reason, must conclude that the purchase price is fair or he or she wouldn't buy the stock. Furthermore, simple logic would dictate that if the company has any value, someone would enter the market at some point to buy at what he or she perceives to be a good price.

Most mutual funds traditionally follow two rules: (1) stay invested, and (2) *only buy* or go long stocks—*never short* them. In other words, mutual fund managers must concentrate on finding those stocks in their particular concentration that will lose the least while markets are going down.

In 2000 and 2001 there was enormous portfolio turnover as mutual fund managers continually dumped poorly performing stocks for less poorly performing issues. In bear markets mutual funds mandated long only have nowhere to hide. Ask any of the managers of the best-performing funds for the five years prior.

Many of these managers were brilliant in their ability to maintain amazing returns year after year during the raging bull market of the nineties. The vast majority of these prodigious funds have since been crushed under the weight of a train coming back down the mountain.

Why would anyone ask to have limited risk controls or limited profit potential? Although you probably don't spend much time driving your car in reverse, you likely wouldn't buy a car that had no reverse. Likewise, only a fraction of time if ever is spent in a car involved in an accident, but consumers demand bumpers, seat belts, and airbags. I live in Colorado in an area that requires four-wheel drive to handle the snow only a couple of weeks per year; yet the opportunity cost, the inability to get to work or school or the grocery store, is such that four-wheel-drive vehicles stay in high demand. When I go into the mountains on a fly-fishing trip or skiing,

I always take one of the four-wheel-drive vehicles. My method for achieving what could be done during the majority of the year with a sedan is modified to fit the situation and to more effectively achieve my intended goal. When market environments change, we must consider other methods for achieving our intended goals. Think like a Marine.

Improvise, Adapt and Overcome

THIS UNOFFICIAL MANTRA OF THE MARINE CORPS IS BASED ON THE FACT
THAT THE CORPS HISTORICALLY RECEIVED ARMY HAND-ME-DOWNS
AND THE TROOPS WERE POORLY EQUIPPED. DESPITE THIS, THE MARINE
CORPS HAS BEEN SUCCESSFUL MOSTLY BECAUSE OF THE CREATIVITY
OF ITS PEOPLE AND THEIR SUCCESS-BASED ATTITUDE.

In the financial markets traders use aphorisms like "Don't fight the tape" and "The trend is your friend" to get the same point across. When markets are going up, you should be long stocks. When markets are going down, you should be short stocks. And when they are going sideways, you should be invested in cash or funds that profit during times of capitulation.

HOW SHORTING CAN IMPROVE PERFORMANCE

A brief note: You need not be a legend to reduce your risk and improve your returns. Common sense, if not reality, mandates that the prudent long-term investor incorporate some form of active risk management. Active risk management will entail some semblance of market timing. Successful managers appreciate the art of designing risk management measures that are appropriate for the investment vehicle and the goals of the investor.

Every investment class, whether it be stock, bond, currency, or mutual fund, has a multitude of personalities. If you have ever raised animals, you know that there are certain traits that run through an entire genus or species. Most domesticated animals bond quickly with their respective caretakers, but cats are not generally as easy to train. Consequently, they are less likely to come running when you call their name; and they tend not to be as adept at Frisbee games. Even so, every dog is not meant to play Frisbee golf.

In just the asset class made up of stocks, some sectors carry volatilities that are regularly four times that of other sectors. Other sectors will see 100 percent changes in their volatility in a single quarter. Though volatility is regularly viewed by managers, especially alternative managers, as a field of opportunity, it is the enemy of the buy-and-hold manager. Where market timers may use swings in stock prices to improve entries and exits, buy-and-hold managers must habitually sit out the storm. Without being precise, market timers and trend followers can outperform the buy-and-hold crowd by short selling into predictable down moves.

SHORT SECRETS OF THE PROS

Funds that are able to hold both long and short positions fall under the heading of long/short funds. Long/short fund managers use varied methodologies and tactics to keep investments predominantly long in bull markets and predominantly short in bear markets. Smart long/short managers recognize that at any given time there are stocks rising and stocks falling. Some use fundamental analysis to identify companies that are prone to rise or fall. Others use pure technical analysis, and still others combine both fundamental and technical analysis.

Finally, selling stocks and other products short brings cash into the account. Though higher margin requirements are generally placed on short positions, the cash is paid interest. That's right. Just as you pay interest when you use margin, you receive interest for holding cash. Institutional hedge fund managers use this strategy regularly to hedge other forms of risk. Income is always a good hedge.

In the currency markets, banks and other large institutions as well as currency traders make use of the "currency carry trade," whereby the currencies of countries with low interest rates are borrowed and exchanged for currencies of countries paying higher interest rates where the funds are deposited. One of the popular trades over the past decade has been to borrow, or short, the Japanese yen while going long, or buying, the Australian dollar. Where the yen may be borrowed at a cost of 0.5 percent per year, the Australian dollar deposit was often paying more than 5 percent.

Another strategy used by professional money managers incorporates the use of options into a short-biased portfolio. One strategy is the simple "writing," or selling, of call options to bring in premium on stock positions that are not expected to rise significantly as a result of a generalized bear market. A more aggressive strategy is the purchasing of put options, whereby profit is made from the *decline* in the underlying security price. Fund managers who are required to maintain a certain percentage of the portfolio long will use this technique to neutralize bear market risk, whereas managers who are able to short may purchase the put options outright rather than shorting the underlying stock.

Managers who are subject to broad market (S&P 500) or index (Biotechnology Index) risk may short the index against their holdings. This eliminates additional cost associated with buying or selling options on specific securities. A large-cap manager wanting to hedge risk or profit from a general downtrend may short the Spyders (SPY) or S&P Index, which are actively traded on the AMEX (American Stock Exchange); while the biotech manager would elect to short the BBH (Merrill Lynch Biotech HOLDRs Trust), which functions like an ETF (exchange-traded fund).

MAKING THE SALE

Where there is movement there is opportunity. Regardless of direction, money can be made in most markets. To limit investing strategies to those that only make money when the price goes up eliminates an important profit center in a well-rounded investment portfolio. Whether shorting stock on your own or allocating funds to a short manager, not only are you opening your portfolio to diversification that is noncorrelated or inversely correlated with most other strategies, but you are widening the field of opportunity for more investments with highly favorable risk-reward ratios.

Those who caution against selling short like to speculate that the stock you short could theoretically go to infinity and you could lose a multiple of your initial investment. Though this concern doesn't come up much with the majority of their clients who use margin and share similar risk, they are still missing the point . . . the big picture. At first glance this appears to be a real concern, especially for those employing only fundamental analysis to assess investments. The astute investor, however, who combines both fundamental and technical analysis is extremely capable of defining the risk and of outlining the appropriate stop-loss measures with short positions in the same way that he or she would with long positions.

Sometimes, becoming accustomed to short selling requires a paradigm shift. In bull markets we look to find the best of the best to leverage the push of the market as it rises. When markets are trending bearish, we look to find the weakest stocks in the weakest sectors to short. Even in sideways markets we can combine these techniques for profit. Once that shift takes place, a new sense of power and control should replace the fear and trepidation. No market can stop you from earning a profit!

Mutual Funds
Are Safe

The concept of a mutual fund is to provide an investor with a broad and actively managed portfolio without the need to do the research required on each entity or to purchase individual shares of each company. In theory, the purchasing power of a fund should keep the relative costs to each investor at a minimum, and the active management by a professional should yield the best possible results. All of this sounds great—kind of like the three musketeers, "All for one and one for all!" And if the rest of the design were not so severely flawed, mutual funds would be everything an investor could hope for.

Sadly, mutual funds in recent years have suffered more from their afflictions than in prior years. This can be attributed to Wall Street's pedagogy endorsing a faulty theory that is just now being realized. Mutual funds take for granted three of the myths previously critiqued. They assume that greater rewards must always be accompanied by greater risk; that the market is the best measuring stick for performance; and that stocks are meant to just buy and hold since the market will carry them all up over time.

Managers at the largest fund companies are routinely compensated for performance as it compares with the market. Little attention is paid when their fund is screaming upward with the market. And what's wrong with rewarding good performance with a hefty bonus? Nothing, of course! The investor wins with great returns, and the manager wins for providing them.

The question is: When a fund loses money, should the manager earn a bonus (not paid mind you, but given a *bonus!*) for losing less than the market? How about for losing less than his or her peers? I don't think so! Fund managers, like anyone else, will have down months, quarters, and even years; and if their losses, or *drawdowns*, are only a fraction of those of their peers, they will in all likelihood have better average and annualized returns than their counterparts over time. Managers and clients alike maintain a more positive outlook when portfolios incur less volatility. But losses are losses. The practice of tacking on an additional expense to an already ailing portfolio is more than an insult to the investor. It is a travesty. This is just another dilemma that has evolved out of the buy-and-hold school of thought.

DRAWDOWN: Reduction in account equity from a trade or series of trades.

If you can only buy and hold, you are very likely going to suffer many negative years interspersed among the profitable ones since the cards are stacked against you in those years. Only in this paradoxical state does rewarding someone for losing your money make sense.

Do you find that you believe most of what you read? Whether that has caused you concern in the past or not, please make sure that you read this a few times:

Absolute returns not relative returns!

You cannot be assured a secure retirement or be guaranteed continued income from *relative returns*.

DON'T BLAME THE FUND MANAGER

One of the great debates of the modern era is that of nature versus nurture. We have argued about the impact that genetics has versus the environment in creating criminals, geniuses, and more. Many assert that certain natural tendencies or predispositions are inherent to a specific genetic makeup.

Without getting too deep into this argument, it can also be said that mutual fund managers are not completely to blame for working within the parameters of a faulty model. Besides being restricted to only the *buy side* of the market and having to focus on beating the indexes, mutual fund managers are charged with staying vested in the market.

> **BUY SIDE:** The part of the financial markets that purchases and sells securities for money-management purposes, rather than for underwriting purposes.

My heart goes out to mutual fund managers who must work under the scrutiny of such mandates. I liken it to the story of Rapunzel. They live in great castles and are well cared for, and yet still they are trapped.

When the markets are ravaging their fund, there is no reprieve to be had by moving to cash; and when the markets are going up, managers must find more investments in which to place the hordes of incoming cash. All of this makes judicious selection more challenging. It is not much better in down markets, when fund managers are forced to liquidate core positions to raise cash for disbursement to nervous investors.

It is something of a catch-22; the better you perform, the more people want to invest. Alternatives for the manager are limited to buying more of what they already own at the risk of becoming overweighted or to finding something new to buy at the risk of lowering the standards followed in the selection of the core portfolio.

Similar problems occur with specialty funds. Specialty funds like those in the telecom and software sectors can amass such huge investor dollars that relative concentrations in individual stock quickly become excessive. When investors, frightened from the volatility, begin withdrawing assets, the funds are forced to sell their holdings to raise the cash. The active selling of such concentrated positions causes the share price to fall even more precipitously.

When mutual funds acquired large share blocks in prior years, their buy-and-hold theory never accounted for times where they would have to sell. Market downturns were meant to buy more, to average in for staggering gains later. Why should there ever be a need to sell outside of some routine profit taking to capitalize new purchases? The conundrum these buy-and-hold managers must all face at some time is the erratic withdrawal of large sums from the fund.

It is rarely an organized response as people are different. They have entered the fund at different times and consequently have different goals for their investments. The pain threshold of investors also varies greatly. Falling markets and fund values drive investors at different levels to begin pulling their assets, intensifying the velocity and downward pressure on the stock.

Clearly the point at which different funds reach critical mass varies immensely. For example, funds that invest in *small-cap* companies are generally more susceptible to the problems associated with large inflows and outflows of cash than funds that invest in *large-cap* companies.

CAPITALIZATION: Companies are usually classified as large cap, medium cap, small cap, or micro cap, depending on their market capitalization, but the dividing lines are somewhat arbitrary. As a general guideline, the market capitalization is $5 billion or more for large caps, $1 billion to $5 billion for medium caps, $250 million to $1 billion for small caps, and less than $250 million for micro caps. When calculating the market caps of a foreign company that has issued American depository receipts (ADRs) in the United States, only the outstanding ADR shares are considered, not the shares issued by that company in other countries.

Managers who originally intended to hold investments for the long term are forced to sell companies whose prices were formerly supported by regular institutional buying. Core holdings for one telecommunications fund are often the same as for other telecom funds. This only exacerbates the problem when times are bad. The die-hard buy-and-hold person who makes no regular adjustments to his or her 401(k) or other retirement plan incurs the full measure of pain.

When investors reared in the ways of buy and hold encounter a real bear market, they can only lie prostrate on the ground and pray that the bear will not eviscerate them like the others. Though the portfolios of many may recover over time, many more will never be restored.

Of lesser importance, but still a valuable consideration when investing in mutual funds, is the propensity for a tax liability occurring in a year when the net asset value has gone down. That is to say, with a mutual fund, you can see the value of your investment in the fund drop, but still owe for capital gains. I began hearing concerns about this problem after the crash of 1987 and then again in the late 1990s.

We often think that tax considerations with mutual funds do not exist, are waived, or at least are somehow better with mutual funds than with other investment vehicles. This is just not true. There are mutual funds that are designed to limit the consequences of capital gains, but most can suffer from this malady. As stocks within a fund begin a general decline, managers must determine whether or not to sell their losers and reinvest in something better or to sell their winners to reinvest (or average down) into their losers. Since mutual funds often buy and hold for long periods, the sale of stock may result in a taxable capital gain that has been created over years—and not necessarily during the time in which you have owned the fund.

So what do the statistics show? A 1996 study by Vanguard found that "out of 273 growth and value funds in operation through the ten years ended December 31, 1995 only 38 funds (14%) beat the compound return on the S&P 500 Index. More important, only 14 funds provided a statistically significant (more than 2%) annual advantage over the Index, while 147 provided significant disadvantage."

When you combine the faults of the buy-and-hold theory with the potential for becoming underdiversified or overdiversified, sprinkle it with tax liability for gains you never realized, and bake it at 350 for about 15 minutes (not 30, as it is only a recipe for a half-baked idea), you should have a mutual fund. Congratulations . . . I think.

My intention in writing this chapter is not to point out what is wrong with mutual funds, but rather to motivate individual investors to take control of their investments and to seek out those investment vehicles that provide logical solutions for achieving short-term and long-term goals. Is there anything else that offers the benefits of a mutual fund without the restrictions that hinder its performance? Of course—and we will cover some of those in the next chapter.

When you put money into a mutual fund, you are hiring that manager to invest those funds to the best of his or her ability. That is quite different from asking him or her to make you money. Over the years I have had discussions with dozens of fund managers who express concern that investors do not truly comprehend this key concept.

A portfolio manager whose mandate is to invest in the Pacific Rim must be committed to uncovering the best of the best in the Pacific Rim. If the economy of those countries falls into the waste basket, the manager's job remains the same. It is our duty as investors to either move our dollars to an area or sector that holds more promise or select an adviser who will be proactive in our stead. If you invest in mutual funds, it is your prerogative— no, it is your obligation—to be proactive about the allocation of your dollars. Think about it. A mutual fund manager will never tell you when to get out of his or her fund.

The increasing demand for proactive assessment and rotation of investment dollars has birthed a group of managers who actively move client holdings in and out of mutual funds in an effort to maximize return and minimize risk. Since there are thousands of mutual funds representing a tremendous selection of sectors and strategies, the idea of moving out of funds that have lost their steam into ones just gaining steam is a powerful concept. One manager I know uses a method called a style box analysis model (SBAM). The essence of the model is the identification of those mutual funds that are beginning a parabolic move upward in the early stages of the move. Once the upward trend has flattened out, the manager looks to sell the fund and purchase another that is just beginning its ascension. Since mutual funds tend to focus on a single sector or strategy, they work well for those who follow the rotation of industry sectors.

My impression is that this concept of market timing for mutual funds is easy to accept for those who have always believed in the fundamental principles behind buy-and-hold and mutual fund investing but want less volatility.

The notion is a good one, but in practice has proved to be riddled with complications. Mutual funds often carry fees and penalties that can add up quickly and dilute performance. To limit activities to funds that charge smaller fees and have no penalties sometimes creates a performance barrier. Regardless, managers using mutual fund–rotation models generally limit transactions to those funds that don't carry these fees. But the dominant issue confronting this manager type is the relationship with the mutual funds themselves.

Many managers who have done well using mutual fund rotation have created a significant rift within the mutual fund companies they trade. Mutual funds tend to relish consistency in their investments and their cash flow. An adviser who repeatedly puts money in and pulls money out of a fund may force the manager into sporadic buying and selling, thereby increasing commission expense and *slippage*.

SLIPPAGE: Slippage is the difference between estimated and actual transaction costs that is generally measured in terms of cents per share in additional cost. This extra expense is common among mutual fund companies that often trade in large blocks of stock that cause the price of the stock to move as a result of the trade magnitude. Some firms specialize in reducing this phenomenon through smart order-routing systems, order-matching services, or a technically savvy trade desk. Efficient entry and exit can result in negative slippage or price improvement.

Some mutual funds have gone so far as to restrict access to managers that they know rotate in and out. Who can blame them? Mutual fund managers are generally buying and holding for the long run. When new money comes in, they put it to work; and when money goes out, they liquidate. The constant inflow and outflow can wreak havoc on a manager's efforts to maintain proper weightings in a fund.

THE ETF ADVANTAGE

Mutual fund timing may continue to prove rewarding to those who overcome the barriers to entry, but the real progress will be made when the same managers find ways to take advantage of bear market trends by using short selling techniques and hedging techniques.

Until that time, the best way to design a portfolio that is built for you is to look into creating a custom portfolio from the various sector funds and ETFs (*exchange-traded funds*) on the market. (For a comparison of mutual funds and exchange-traded funds, see Exhibit 5–1.) These electronically traded entities are in fact gaining in popularity since they lack the costs associated with managing and operating a mutual fund. The annual expense ratio of an ETF is typically a fraction of a standard mutual fund due to reduced marketing, distribution, and accounting expense. Consequently, most index ETFs do not impose annual 12b-1 fees.

EXCHANGE-TRADED FUNDS (ETFS): These funds are baskets of securities, generally stocks or bonds, that track highly recognized indexes. They are similar to mutual funds, except they trade in real time on an exchange rather than requiring purchasers to buy at an end-of-day valuation or NAV (net asset value). Unlike a mutual fund, an index ETF is created when an institutional investor deposits securities into the fund in return for creation units. In return for the deposit, the institutional investor receives a fixed amount of shares, some or all of which may be traded and priced continuously throughout the day on a stock exchange. Exchange-traded equity funds and exchange-traded fixed-income funds are offered as well. Active traders are attracted to ETFs because they trade like a stock. Longer-term traders and investors are moving toward ETFs because of the extremely low management fees and tax advantages.

Mutual Funds versus Exhange-Traded Funds

	Mutual Funds	Exchange-Traded Funds
Research	Heavy	None
Research expense	Heavy	None
Administration expense	High	Moderate
Management expense	Varies	Low
Tax inefficiencies	Yes	No
Load fees	Yes	No
Commission fees	No	Yes
Intraday trading	No	Yes
Promote active trading	No	Yes
Good for dollar cost avg.	Yes	Only with larger dollars
Good for buy and hold	Yes	Yes

EXHIBIT 5-1

Since index ETFs are passively managed (you are the active part) and seek only to follow a specific index, they generally realize fewer capital gains than actively managed funds. Investors may also receive in-kind redemptions, where they receive stock instead of cash, and may sell the shares at their leisure. More importantly, the fund itself does not suffer from the redemption, where as a mutual fund would be subject to capital gains on securities sold to provide for the investor's redemption.

HOW TO FIND THE FUNDS FOR YOU

There can be a measurable difference between actively managed mutual funds and index funds or ETFs. At present, an ideal portfolio would likely include sector funds offered from a firm like Fidelity, actively managed index funds through a firm like Vanguard, and ETFs offered on the major U.S. exchanges. Below are some of the largest ETF groups and ETF products:

DIAMONDS. The Diamonds Trust Series 1, an ETF that tracks the Dow Jones Industrial Average and is structured as a unit investment trust.

iSHARES. A group of ETFs advised and marketed by Barclays Global Investors. i-Shares are structured as open-end mutual funds.

HOLDRs. Holding company depository receipts, a type of ETF marketed by Merrill Lynch. Unlike other ETFs, HOLDRs can only be bought and sold in 100-share increments. HOLDRs do not have creation units like other ETFs, but investors may exchange 100 shares of a HOLDR for its underlying stocks at any time. Existing HOLDRs focus on narrow industry groups. Each initially owns 20 stocks, but the HOLDRs are unmanaged and so can become more concentrated due to mergers or to the disparate performance of their holdings.

QUBES (QQQ). The NASDAQ 100 tracking stock, an ETF that tracks the technology-laden NASDAQ 100 index. The popular name, Qubes, derives from the ETF's ticker symbol, QQQ. Qubes are structured as unit investment trusts. Qubes are by far the most heavily traded ETF.

SPIDERS (SPDRS). The Standard & Poors' depository receipts, a group of ETFs that track a variety of Standard & Poors' indexes. The SPDR Trust,

Series 1, usually referred to as "Spiders," tracks the S&P 500 Index. Select Sector SPDRs track various sector indexes that carve up the S&P 500 Index into separate industry groups. SPDR Trust, Series 1, is structured as a unit investment trust, but Select Sector SPDRs are open-end funds.

STREETTRACKS. A group of ETFs managed by State Street Global Advisors. These ETFs track various indexes, including Dow Jones–style specific and global indexes, technology indexes from Morgan Stanley Dean Witter, and the Wilshire REIT index. StreetTracks are open-end funds, not unit investment trusts, and trade on the American Stock Exchange.

VIPERS. The Vanguard Index Participation Receipts—the ETF versions of several Vanguard index funds. VIPERs are structured as share classes of existing open-end funds. The only VIPER currently available is the Vanguard Total Stock Market VIPER, but Vanguard plans to launch others.

A basic strategy for building a portfolio around ETFs and sector-based funds begins with the creation of a table of funds that cover the major markets, industries, and sectors that you wish to cover. This process is extremely important, as it sets the universe for which selections will be made. The clearer the delineations you make between the various funds, the more useful they will be during the selection process.

As you create the universe of funds, make note of the average volatility of the fund over the previous quarter and over the previous year. Though volatility is not always bad, it is important to track for all investments. Also include the performance for at least the past quarter, six months, and year. If you intend to be very active, you may also want to look at what has happened over the past month. The last piece for a simple review is to compare the correlations of each fund. The correlation is a measure illustrating how closely two securities are related. Highly correlated funds will tend to move in similar patterns over time, while funds with low correlations tend to respond to different factors. This does not mean that all the sectors going up at any given time are closely related or correlated, though closely correlated securities do tend to follow this pattern. The goal of diversification among the funds is a blend of funds with low correlations that are all covering markets, industries, and/or sectors that are tracking upward. Using basic support and resistance and moving-average trendlines, you can maintain a portfolio of funds that are always tracking upward. In those instances where there just don't seem to be appropriate selections, move assets to cash. Your capital will remain preserved for the times when trends are more evident.

Managers who do not adhere to the limitations of the buy-and-hold philosophy can reduce volatility and improve performance with good fundamental and technical analysis. As active managers continue to embrace alternatives to the mutual funds of old, market-driven tradable indexes will become more and more valuable to everyone. Over time the buy-and-hold crowd will likely be outperformed by the ETFs, or they will simply experience greater volatility to arrive at the same end. You can achieve the results you want and deserve by employing these simple techniques.

All Funds Are
Created Equal

I t should be clear by now that there is plenty to choose from in the world of investing. ETFs are redefining the way we look at the markets. But the real revolution in today's financial arena comes from the area of alternative investments. The impact that these innovative investment vehicles are already having is astonishing. Even a short dissertation on the merits of *alternative investments* in today's evolving investment climate necessitates a brief history.

ALTERNATIVE INVESTMENTS: Alternative investments are those investments that have historically been specialty products offered only to sophisticated investors and encompassing a full array of subjects and vehicles, including real estate, precious metals, commodities, futures, private equity, oil and gas, timber, and hedge funds, to name only a few. Though the term *alternative* has sometimes carried negative connotations, institutions and high-net-worth individuals have embraced these types of investments for many decades.

WHY THE WORLD'S WEALTHIEST USE ALTERNATIVES

Where the buy-and-hold crowd of money managers have, to date, eschewed the alternative investment arena, the smart money has been there for years. Like any investment vehicle, alternative investments may possess risks that are not found in simple equity or mutual fund investing. Oftentimes, however, tremendous opportunity can be found with less risk and volatility.

> **HEDGE FUND:** A fund, historically usually used by wealthy individuals and institutions, which is allowed to use aggressive strategies that are unavailable to mutual funds, including selling short, leverage, program trading, swaps, arbitrage, and derivatives. Hedge funds are exempt from many of the rules and regulations governing other mutual funds, which promotes their efficiency in accomplishing specific investing goals. They are restricted by law to no more than 100 investors per fund, and as a result most hedge funds set high minimum investment amounts, ranging anywhere from $10,000 to over $1 million. As with traditional mutual funds, investors in hedge funds pay a management fee; however, hedge funds also collect a percentage of the profits (usually 20–25 percent). Hedge fund managers are much more likely to be focused on absolute return than mutual funds managers, and incentive bonuses are generally paid only on new profits.

One of the most lucrative areas for investing in today's market may be in *hedge funds*. Over the past decade, the typical hedge fund has produced risk-adjusted returns similar to that of mutual funds, but the performance values have tended to be more favorable (see Exhibit 6–1). Without the limitations of style and strategy, the world of hedge funds will likely continue its diverse growth. In a study done by a team at Morgan Stanley Dean Witter entitled "Why Hedge Funds Make Sense" (by Michael W. Peskin, Michael S. Urias, Satish I. Anjilvel, and Bryen E. Boudreau, *Quantitative Strategies*, November 2000), substantial evidence was given for "the superior risk-adjusted performance of indexes of hedge funds as compared to traditional active managers and passive benchmarks." The same study noted that "the volatility of hedge fund indexes is typically much lower than that of mutual fund indexes and equity benchmarks. This is because of the low correlation among individual hedge funds."

Hedge Fund Performance

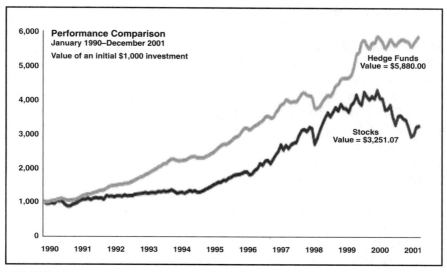

EXHIBIT 6-1

THE HEDGE FUND ADVANTAGE

The team of experts at Morgan Stanley Dean Witter were so convinced of the role of hedge funds in strategic asset allocation that they went on to recommend this class of alternative investment for inclusion in pension plans and endowment funds. Likely, they based their opinion on the substantial data suggesting there is an inherent risk-averse nature among hedge fund managers as well as a performance history that is robust even in bear markets. The extraordinary success had by hedge funds is often said to be based on their exploitation of market inefficiencies. This may well be true; and as markets grow in size along with the number of participants and the number of instruments available for trade, it appears that opportunity will continue to abound.

Hedge funds are not categorized in the same fashion as traditional funds. Many are more specific in their purpose or design. Just as hedge funds are distinctly different in their general design and intent than traditional mutual funds, there are tremendous differences among each of the hedge fund styles. Some may or may not hedge against market downturns, though most aim to reduce volatility and risk while attempting to preserve capital and deliver positive (absolute) returns under all market conditions. Below is a list of the major hedge fund styles:

AGGRESSIVE GROWTH. This fund style seeks investments in equities that are expected to experience acceleration in the growth of earnings per share. Stocks purchased for aggressive growth generally have high P/E ratios, have low or no dividends, and in some cases are small-cap and micro-cap stocks that are expected to experience rapid growth. This style also includes sector specialist funds such as technology, banking, or biotechnology. Aggressive growth managers hedge by shorting equities where earnings disappointment is expected or by shorting stock indexes. These managers do tend to carry a long bias. Volatility is typically *high*.

DISTRESSED SECURITIES. The distressed manager buys equity or buys debt of companies at deep discounts. Typically these companies are facing bankruptcy or reorganization. Managers tend to have a highly specialized background in banking, accounting, or mergers and acquisitions. Distressed managers seek to profit from the market's knack for overselling the stock of weak companies. The number crunching and due diligence required pose a giant hurdle for the regular investor, but they are the bread and butter of the distressed manager. Institutional investors, like mutual funds, are often restricted from owning securities that are not "investment grade." They must sell whether they want to own the stock or not. Once these securities rebound, institutions can propel them quickly upward. Markets rebounding after a sustained bear market generally reward distressed managers with an extra boost, though results are usually not dependent on the direction of the markets. Volatility is typically *low to moderate.*

EMERGING MARKETS. These funds invest in the equity or debt of emerging markets. Some focus on markets in, say, Latin America or Eastern Europe, while others go wherever perceived opportunity exists. These countries or regions often have higher inflation and volatile growth. Short selling is not permitted in many emerging markets, and, therefore, effective hedging is often not available. Brady debt, debt issued by the governments of developing countries, can be partially hedged via U.S. Treasury futures and currency markets. Volatility can be *very high.*

FUNDS OF HEDGE FUNDS. A fund of funds uses a mix and match of other hedge funds and other pooled investment vehicles. This blending of different strategies and asset classes aims to provide a more stable long-term investment return than any of the individual funds. Returns, risk, and volatility can be controlled by the mix of underlying strategies and funds. Capital preservation is generally an important consideration. Some funds of funds are specialized, investing in groups of technology managers or arbitrage managers. Others focus on specific geographic regions. Funds of funds may be widely diversified, or they may be quite focused. The fund of funds is rapidly becoming a staple in the portfolios of pension funds, endowments, insurance companies, private banks, and high-net-worth individuals. Volatility depends on the mix and ratio of strategies employed but is generally *low*.

INCOME. The primary focus of the income manager is yield or current income. Some managers may use leverage to buy bonds or derivatives in order to increase interest income or to leverage potential principal appreciation derived from favorable price changes. The extent of leverage used is a key determinant in the style of income managers. Regardless of approach, most income funds have an expected volatility that is *low*.

GLOBAL MACRO. This specific approach aims to profit from changes in global economies, typically brought about by shifts in government policy that impact interest rates, in turn affecting currency, stock, and bond markets. The term macro comes from the "macroeconomic" view taken by these managers. Since global macro managers depend on large general trends to profit, they typically use leverage both to hedge and to increase exposure in particular markets. Global macro managers typically participate in all the major world markets and use most major securities, including equities, bonds, currencies, and commodities, to gain an edge. Global macro funds were made famous by investors like George Soros who stay away from specific stocks (unlike investors such as Warren Buffett) in favor of much larger trends. Though leverage is used both directionally and as a hedge, the directional investments are where returns are expected. Consequently volatility is *very high*.

MARKET NEUTRAL—ARBITRAGE. The arbitrage manager attempts to hedge out most market risk by taking offsetting positions, often in different securities of the same issuer. For example, he or she may be long convertible bonds and short the underlying equity. He or she may also use futures to hedge out interest rate risk. The primary focus of the market neutral—arbitrage manager lies in obtaining returns with very low correlation to both the equity and bond markets. These relative-value strategies include fixed-income arbitrage, mortgage-backed securities, capital structure arbitrage, and closed-end fund arbitrage. The volatility of these risk-averse funds is generally *very low.*

MARKET NEUTRAL—EQUITY. These managers try to remain as close to being perfectly hedged as possible through combined investments in long and short equity positions that are equal in dollar value and are in the same sectors of the market. Market risk is greatly reduced, but effective stock analysis and stock picking are essential to obtaining meaningful results. Leverage may be used to enhance returns. Market-neutral—equity managers often use a strategy called pairs trading, whereby they track the normal trend and relationship between two or more equities in the same sector in an effort to take advantage of disparities in pricing. These managers sometimes use market index futures to hedge out systematic (market) risk. Performance and volatility are often compared to U.S. T-bills though the models are typically not correlated. Volatility is generally *low.*

MARKET TIMING. There are a plethora of strategies used by market timers with wide ranging expertise. Oftentimes the allocation of funds among different asset classes is dependent on the manager's view of the economic or market outlook. There is a rising popularity among market-timing managers employing technical analysis to define trends and countertrends in the market. The portfolio emphasis may swing widely between asset classes. There are as many strategies in this style as there are managers. As a result, volatility varies, though it is regularly *moderate to high.*

OPPORTUNISTIC. The investment theme changes from strategy to strategy as opportunities arise to profit from events such as IPOs, sudden price changes often caused by an interim earnings disappointment, hostile bids, and other event-driven opportunities. The opportunistic manager may utilize several of these investing styles at a given time and is not restricted to any particular investment approach or asset class. One subspecialty is convertible arbitrage. Managers in these styles seek to take advantage of temporary price inefficiencies by taking both long and short positions in related securities. Volatility, though variable, is typically *moderate.*

MULTISTRATEGY. The investment approach of the multistrategy manager may involve minimal or extensive diversification. The concept of the multistrategy model is to be diversified by employing various strategies simultaneously to realize short- and long-term gains. Other strategies may include trend following, counter trend, and various other diversified technical strategies. This style of investing allows the manager to overweight or underweight different strategies to best capitalize on current investment opportunities. Depending on the strategies utilized by the manager, expected volatility may range from *low to high.*

SHORT SELLING. The short selling manager shorts securities in anticipation of being able to purchase them at a future date at a lower price due to a declining price trend. The manager's assessment of the overvaluation of the securities, or the market, or in anticipation of earnings disappointments due to accounting irregularities, new competition, change of management, etc., gives fundamental cause to consider shorting. Managers who incorporate strict technical analysis guidelines and risk management may significantly reduce portfolio volatility though expected volatility in a short-only fund is typically *high.*

SPECIAL SITUATIONS. These managers invest where event-driven situations such as mergers, hostile takeovers, reorganizations, or leveraged buyouts create pricing discrepancies. Some managers in this style incorporate the simultaneous purchase of stock in companies being acquired and the sale of stock in its acquirer (merger arbitrage), hoping to profit from the spread between the current market price and the ultimate purchase price of the company. Special-situations managers typically use leverage and derivatives to enhance returns and to hedge out interest rate and market risk. This investment style is typically noncorrelated to the general market. Volatility also tends to be *low to moderate.*

VALUE. The value manager invests in securities perceived to be selling at deep discounts to their intrinsic or potential worth. Such securities may be out of favor or have minimal following by analysts. Some managers in this style who were trained on Wall Street use only fundamentals to make purchasing decisions and often end up waiting for long periods of time to see results. Performance for these managers comes as a result of maintaining a stable of high-potential issues. Those value managers that do use technical analysis must still use patience and great discipline to hold positions until an opportune value can be realized from the market. Volatility in these funds is generally *low to moderate.*

SPECIALTY FUNDS

As mentioned earlier, hedge funds are often managed by individuals with an expertise in a specific area or market. In recent years, the tremendous demand for these alternative funds has spawned an even more specialized class of funds. The malleable nature of hedge funds allows managers with any number of strategies to transform each investment vehicle into a custom creation. Typical specialities include:

ENERGY. Some investments, such as oil and gas, are undergoing metamorphic changes such that they more closely resemble well-diversified energy portfolios. Leading the charge are firms like Energy Exploration Management, LLC (EEM), which combine vertical and horizontal drilling operations across varied geographies with investments in renewable energy projects such as geothermal, wind, solar, hydroelectric, and other "green" sources. The old-fashioned method of investing in a single oil-drilling project historically resulted in concentrated risk and returns with an inherent decline curve. Now, experienced energy experts like Richard Buccelato and Donald Schwarz of EEM are teaming up and cutting out the expensive up-front costs and middleman expenses and going straight to the investor. This kind of one-stop-shop solution for investors wanting a "pure energy play" is sure to replace the less efficient choices in the coming years.

   In addition to diversification, investors can look for returns to continue for decades due to a significant portion of profits being rolled back into the new investments. Investor-friendly funds like this are being launched in record numbers.

REAL ESTATE. Real estate is a standard holding in the portfolios of most institutions, because as Will Rogers said, "They don't make any more of the stuff." Investing in accounts that own real estate can be particularly useful in building retirement assets. First, real estate returns sometimes run counter to both stocks and bonds and can therefore help diversify your portfolio. Second, property values and rental income have traditionally tended to parallel inflation, so real estate holdings can help protect your future purchasing power. And since values tend to rise and fall more slowly than stock and bond prices, real estate can help reduce your portfolio's volatility. Special government regulations have been put into place for funds created specifically for investing in real estate called *REITs*.

REAL ESTATE INVESTMENT TRUST (REIT): A REIT is a company dedicated to owning and, in most cases, operating income-producing real estate such as apartments, shopping centers, offices, and warehouses. Some REITs also are engaged in financing real estate. Most importantly, to be a REIT a company is legally required to pay virtually all of its taxable income (90 percent) to its shareholders every year.

The benefit of the REIT is that it may deduct the dividends paid to the shareholders from its corporate tax bill so long as the company's assets consist primarily of long-term real estate holdings, income is derived from real estate, and the company pays out at least 90 percent of its taxable income to shareholders. Private (not publicly traded) REITS are becoming more popular as investors seek exposure in specific areas, and the customized returns are available through the purchase of targeted properties.

FACTORING. Companies that run a manufacturing or service business are often subject to payments being sent long after products or services have been given to the customer. When cash flow is tight, this creates a problem. Even when sales are going through the roof, cash flow can be a problem. Factoring firms serve this area by providing short-term loans to companies, which use receivables as security. Most factoring firms take assignment of the associated future payments so that payments are sent directly to them. Generally, the company using the factoring service is loaned the principal amount minus a small percentage for the service. Loaning the same dollars again and again can add up for the factoring firm, and investments (loans) are backed by the receivables. Private funds utilizing factoring services are emerging around the world. In the United States, the factoring of medical bills for hospitals and physician practices is seeing the most rampant growth.

SECURED DEBT. When times are good, people use their credit cards. When times are bad, they use them even more. Credit has become such a standard that individuals and families are almost expected to use credit. There are always people who are going through hard times and fail to pay their credit card bills. Credit card companies write off more than a billion dollars per month in the United States alone, and the numbers in other countries continue to grow as well. Firms like Austin-based Collins Financial Services purchase the written-off debt for pennies on the dollar and then put into action a combination of efforts to obtain the nearly forgotten funds. Walt

Collins and his team have it down to a science. They work with individuals to set up reasonable payment plans and to reestablish their credit. Those who are more indignant are typically approached by one of a hundred nationwide legal eagles specializing in debtor law. This business is growing, and specialty funds built around this type of operation may be considered noncorrelated to the broad markets, if not inversely correlated.

MANAGED FUTURES. In the world of derivatives, managed futures are king. Former floor traders and technical analysts around the globe have been offering their wares for decades. Many of these managers are quickly swept up by larger hedge fund groups or private entities wanting the huge profits that they often produce. The variety of strategies in managed futures is vast. It is common among managers of futures-based funds to combine the strategies of multiple managers where their background or expertise has created a unique insight into a particular substrategy.

AUTOMATED SYSTEMS. The advent of computer-based modeling, genetic algorithms, and artificial intelligence has created a demand for systems that remove the element of human emotion. Some of these systems work exceptionally well, though many are limited in their ability to handle large sums of money. Most funds running automated systems typically incorporate the expertise of mathematicians, technical analysts, and computer programmers. The popularity of this style of fund has grown exponentially over the past decade due to its inherent dependence on strong position and risk management. Strategies that have been incorporated into this investment class include momentum, arbitrage, trend following, and countertrending. One market or multiple markets may be included in a single strategy. Investors interested in pursuing this class of investment are advised to obtain special training in the nuances of computer-aided models. Volatility varies widely depending on the specific strategy used, but most tend to be moderate.

As you can see, the selection among hedge funds is tremendous, without even considering the many subspecialties. Their popularity is increasing their demand, and with demand comes more product selection.

Hedge funds have, in fact, seen record growth over the past decade. Moreover, when markets turned south in 2000, hedge funds were given an additional boost as the comparative performance gap widened. (See Exhibit 6–2.)

During the last 15 years, the S&P 500 Index has had 15 negative quarters, totaling a negative return of 108.1 percent. During those negative quarters, the average U.S. equity mutual fund had a total negative return of 111.8

Hedge Funds Outperform Mutual Funds
in Falling Equity Markets

	S&P 500	VAN U.S. Hedge Fund Index	Morningstar Average Equity Mutual Fund
1Q90	−3%	2.20%	−2.80%
3Q90	−13.70%	−3.70%	−15.40%
2Q91	−0.20%	2.30%	−0.90%
1Q92	−2.50%	5.00%	−0.70%
1Q94	−3.80%	−0.80%	−3.20%
4Q94	−0.02%	−1.20%	−2.60%
3Q98	−9.90%	−6.10%	−15.00%
3Q99	−6.20%	2.10%	−3.20%
2Q00	−2.70%	0.30%	−3.60%
3Q00	−1.00%	3.00%	0.60%
4Q00	−7.80%	−2.40%	−7.80%
1Q01	−11.90%	−1.10%	−12.70%
3Q01	−14.70%	−3.80%	−17.20%
2Q02	−13.40%	−1.40%	−10.70%
3Q02	−17.30%	−3.60%	−16.60%
Total	−108.12%	−9.20%	−111.80%

EXHIBIT 6-2

percent, while the average hedge fund had a total negative return of only 9.2 percent. This clearly demonstrates the ability of hedge funds to preserve capital in falling equity markets.

Hedge funds on average have enjoyed stronger performance over most time frames for a variety of reasons. One reason may be that hedge funds link manager remuneration to fund performance (absolute positive performance). Many of these managers tend to be heavily invested in their own funds and know that they will share in the risks and the rewards with the investors. Some of the confidence of these managers may be due to the fact that most are highly specialized or have a unique expertise. While this may be a little intimidating to some, the best and brightest on Wall Street are leaving in droves from the confines of the mutual fund warehouses, to prove their worth as hedge fund managers.

Another reason that these alternative funds fare better in bad times can be found in their ability to utilize a multitude of financial instruments to reduce risk and enhance returns. Many incorporate tools like short selling, options, futures, currencies, and more to streamline performance. Though there is a popular misconception that all hedge funds are highly volatile, the facts just don't bear this out as truth. In fact, the most volatile of the hedge fund strategies has historically been among managers employing a global macro approach where longer-term directional movements in specific indexes, currencies, bonds, and commodities are combined with high leverage. The global macro fund strategies are far more volatile than typical hedge fund strategies and make up less than 5 percent of all hedge funds.

There are an estimated 7000+ hedge funds in the world today, with assets of more than $500 billion. Current trends put assets in these funds at more than $1 trillion by the end of the decade. All estimates are for hedge funds to grow on a global basis as more *accredited investors* discover this new asset class.

ACCREDITED INVESTOR: Any natural person whose individual net worth or joint net worth with that person's spouse, at the time of the purchase, exceeds $1 million.

Any natural person who had individual income in excess of $200,000 in each of the two most recent years or joint income with that person's spouse in excess of $300,000 in each of those years and has a reasonable expectation of reaching the same income level in the current year.

Any trust with total assets in excess of $5 million, not formed for the specific purpose of acquiring the securities offered, whose purchase of the securities is directed by a person who has such knowledge and experience in financial and business matters that he or she is capable of evaluating the merits and risks of the prospective investment.

Any organization that was not formed for the purpose of acquiring the securities being sold and with total assets in excess of $5 million.

Any director, executive officer, or general partner of the issuer of the securities being offered or sold, or any director, executive officer, or general partner of a general partner of that issuer.

And any entity in which all of the equity owners are accredited investors.

ANYONE CAN BUILD A GREAT ALTERNATIVE PORTFOLIO

For those who are not accredited, there is hope. The demand for better performance and diversification is creating a swell of support that will have to be reconciled by the regulatory boards and agencies. The recent popularity of hedge funds has brought about more interest from regulatory organizations for sure. It is likely that increased oversight of hedge funds will come to pass through either new regulations or the implementation of practice standards. As self-regulatory agencies are put in place and standards of practice are established and embraced, I would expect the barriers to entry for individuals and small businesses into this phenomenal investment class to be lowered dramatically. For everything ranging from personal portfolios to IRAs, SEPs, and 401(k)s, the average investor has been the most victimized by the flawed design and overly restrictive nature of mutual funds. In the interest of providing equal access to the masses, the most appropriate changes in hedge fund regulation are those that make these investment vehicles more readily available.

Before the boom in hedge funds began in the last part of the twentieth century as part of a flight to safety, individual investors were clamoring for the returns that were found in the alternative investment universe. This demand has in turn stimulated a wave of intense growth in managed account programs (MAPs) and separately managed accounts (SMAs). Rather than providing a temporary solution to a market crying out for alternative managers, these simple-to-set-up accounts may soon become the industry standard.

When compared with other alternatives, managed accounts offer significant value to investors. It may be that we as individuals just like to be treated special, or it may be that we really believe that our goals will be better met if our investments are personalized. Managed accounts may be individually tailored to meet the specific needs and objectives of investors. Comprehensive questionnaires are generally completed by each investor to assess specific investment goals and to obtain an optimal blend of money managers for achieving those goals. Interestingly, most of the services offered to hedge fund investors are now standard for managed account programs. Some of the services provided include a written investment policy statement, a comprehensive risk-disclosure document, monthly performance reports, and professional oversight of each account.

Managed accounts are held in the name of the investor, and securities are purchased specifically for that account without the investor commingling or pooling funds with other investors. Technology has improved so dramatically in the past decade, that managers who were reticent to take on the responsibility of multiple accounts are discovering that execution and clearing platforms have made almost anything possible. A single click can purchase a security that can then be split evenly across all accounts automatically in real time. The ability to buy in large quantities and then split up each trade improves efficiency, and individual investors benefit from the lower fees. Moreover, the account cannot be adversely affected by the accounts of others and cannot suffer a tax liability for past performance as with mutual funds. In 2000, mutual fund investors were soaked for $345 billion in capital gains distributions in a year where the average equity fund *lost* 4.5 percent.[*]

FOLLOW THE SMART MONEY

The managed account may be funded with cash or securities, and in some programs notional funds may be used and varying degrees of leverage may be selected so that risk and reward are in line with the investor's interests.

Assets held in separately managed accounts grew from $75 billion industrywide in 1994 to more than $415 billion in 2001. Estimates are for these individualized account programs to more than double, reaching more than a trillion dollars in aggregate by 2008. Also, accounts may be designed to reflect the personal values of the investor. Stephen Bolt, a leader in the world of values-based investing and CEO of Faith Financial Planners, noted recently that "individual investors, foundations, endowments, and most other charitable groups are redefining their investment policies to insure that investment decisions reflect the goals of the organization." Managed account programs give individuals and organizations a measure of customization that cannot be found in a mutual fund.

Through the inclusion of hedge funds and managed accounts in your portfolio, you will be bringing in management that looks to achieve what you want to achieve, absolute returns. Before jumping into anything new, make sure that you study and compare strategies, styles, and managers. Get used to reading the documentation that these managers are required to provide by law. Where some managers charge a 1 percent management fee per annum for assets under management and an incentive fee of 20 percent of

---

[*]Lauricella and O'Brian: "Getting Personal: Popularity of Managed Accounts Grows," April 5, 2001, *The Wall Street Journal*, Dow Jones, Inc.

net new profits (often referred to as 1 and 20), other managers may charge a 2 percent management fee and a 25 percent incentive fee. Don't be afraid to pay for quality, as many of these managers are deserving of their rates— but do your due diligence on the strategy and the manager before investing. Even in the world of hedge funds, past performance is not always a guarantee of future results.

C H A P T E R

IPOs Are Easy Money

There's gold in them thar hills!
—CRUSTY OLD GUY, 1849

IPOs, or initial public offerings, may not be the lifeblood of an economy or even a market, but they are certainly an indicator demonstrating the vitality of both. Like the forty-niners digging for gold or the wildcatters looking for oil, finding great IPOs is dependent on the quality of research done ahead of time. The actual purchase and sale of the IPO should be the reward for a job well done.

What is an IPO? It is simply the first sale of stock by a company to the public. A company can raise money by issuing debt in the form of bonds or by selling equity ownership in the form of shares of stock. If the company has never issued equity (sold ownership shares) to the public, the first offering to the public is known as an initial public offering. Any sale or issuance of equity by the company to the public thereafter is referred to as a secondary offering.

IPOs IN THE 1990s

In the bull market of the 1990s, new IPOs were the talk of the town. Hardly a discussion was held at the water cooler or at a cocktail party without the news of the latest and greatest companies "going public." These offerings regularly saw stellar moves on their first day, and dozens upon dozens rocketed upward for weeks and months afterward. The multitude of winning IPO plays overshadowed the relatively few failures. But as markets slowed down, so did the IPO deal flow. Fewer *syndicates* could be launched with the confidence to launch a new company into the investor pool when equity markets were falling so dramatically. But IPOs can still put you as an investor at a strategic advantage if you are savvy enough to know where to look and if you are equipped with the right information.

> **SYNDICATE:** A group of bankers, insurers, and brokers who work together for the purpose of sharing the risk associated with supporting or underwriting large loans or initial public offerings.

One of the world's foremost experts in the field of initial public offerings and related offerings is David Menlow, the founder and CEO of IPOfinancial.com. Mr. Menlow has been in the industry for more than a decade and was one of the first in the market to aggregate the reams of information in a single place for the IPO investor. In a recent discussion, I had the opportunity to garner some wonderful insights from Mr. Menlow. The highlights from that interview are shared below.

RL: What is the real value for investors in the IPO market? How is it different from other forms of investing?

DM: Traditional investments in IPOs are typically about gaining value through long-term capital gains. It is supposedly about taking a good idea with good management and a good product or service and accelerating its growth through the infusion of public funds directly into the heart of a company. What can really send a company into financial orbit is this cash infusion that allows them to de-leverage the balance sheet, which in turn allows them to create an acquisition currency. This ultimately enables the company to grow inorganically through the creation of stock that can be used to acquire other companies or to add to the company resources to grow the company internally. In this case it is much like the company being hit with a defibrillator. This is a kind of a financial defibrillator with the exception that the patient here is an already healthy company.

RL: How much of the supercharged capacity is being initiated or accounted for by the initial pricing of the IPO? To what degree is the valuation representative of a forward-looking bias versus one that is more representative of the company's present value?

DM: The general thinking is that underwriters have to do their job in the pricing model of the IPO to achieve the delicate balance whereby the issuing company can receive the appropriate dollar infusion while also allowing for somewhat of a discount in the shares when compared with similar companies in the sector or industry as incentive for the buyers of the IPO stock. This is done irrespective of what conditions exist within the entire sector at any given time. By that I mean, we may be looking at companies with a significant reduction in their P/E [price-to-earnings ratio]; and if the company is being priced during this time, we would want to see more evidence for the company to carry a valuation that would be closer to the rest of the companies in the sector. Additionally, if the entire sector is carrying a high valuation, the underwriters may find that to find an appropriate valuation is a bit simpler, but the stock must still carry a price that is at a discount to the rest of the sector. In any case, it is always about present-day pricing fundamentals. But if the sector is regularly valued using forward looking pricing models, the IPO would also be valued using a similar model.

RL: A few years ago we would see stocks double in the first few days. We used to wonder if the CEOs were muttering under their breath about the underwriters' leaving money on the table for underpricing the offering. Why didn't the underwriters price the company higher and let the company take in those dollars rather than leave those dollars in the public sector?

DM: I have always been on record as saying that underwriters in general have done an extraordinarily good job of pricing new issues. To price any IPO to the levels of demand is a recipe for disaster, and that [demand] is what caused the huge disparity in the marketplace. For example, the highest first-day gain of any IPO was VA Linux systems (LNUX) with a 733 percent first-day gain on December 9, 1999; and TheGlobe.com (TGLO) with 606 percent in November of 1998 was not far behind. But these companies, had they been priced to demand, would have created a one-way street of benefit directly to the issuing company, and the resulting lawsuits that would have ensued following the decline of these stocks would have put the brokerage business collectively out of business.

RL: So where you hear about the perforation of the Chinese wall and the pushing of stocks with an IPO with a PE of 1800, do you feel the pricing of an IPO is generally more conservative simply because of the nature of the pricing models?

DM: The pricing of these deals must be done with some semblance of a pricing model, because if at some point there was a huge drop-off in the price of the stock without the stock having ever really seen upward movement, teams of lawyers would jump on the issuers, questioning the reason and the standard for the pricing. If they [the underwriters] responded that they were pricing to demand, it would be an open and shut case. Though there must certainly have been temptation, most underwriters were very bold in pricing the IPOs using a respectable model. It just so happened that the markets provided very fertile ground both for the secondary market and for corruption. From *laddering* to a variety of other strategies, corruption was very prominent in the secondary market. Underwriters knew that they had a very desirable product, and as a result of the wide disparities in the IPO price and the prices in the aftermarket, there was tremendous opportunity for inappropriate behavior.

LADDERING: Laddering generally involves the promotion of inflated pre-IPO prices for the sake of obtaining a greater allotment of an offering. Typically an illegal practice, some investment banks would encourage clients to buy additional shares in companies after their IPO in exchange for larger initial allocations of IPO shares.

RL: Do you think there has been a lot of change in the IPO market or the perception of IPO investing in the past two decades?

DM: I think that there is a greater level of information now available to the IPO investor. I know that our company was founded on the theory that we were going to break out of the good ol' boy network. In fact, when we started 14 years ago, it was about allowing the retail investor, the individual investor, to get information in advance of the institutions. I say that because we were able to bring the valuable information that investors really needed to make decisions by doing independent research. At that time, information was difficult to come by, as information was generally only shared if there was something you could offer in turn, and people could only find out about IPOs if they had some special relationship. Now the information is better and more readily available through services like ours which allows the individual investor access to research independent of the issuing firms and selling broker-dealers. The biggest difference in today and yesterday is the playing field. Investors now have the opportunity to invest on a level playing field by using the same information that is used by institutional investors.

RL: In your opinion what myths still exist regarding the IPO market?

DM: One of the greatest myths still out there is that there is equal access to the actual IPOs themselves. There is often a very limited supply for almost an unlimited demand, and this kind of imbalance can lead to levels of perversion in the sales practices of the brokerage firms. The decision is still left to the individual broker; and if the broker has a demand for 30,000 shares, the broker does not seek to win the Nobel Prize for his fairness or his magnanimous nature. He will generally look to the clients who do the most business or generate the most commissions or bring in the most referrals or what have you. For all the legislations that have surfaced, and with all the decisions and fines that have been handed down, this is still a rigged game.

RL: From where does the generalization that "all IPOs are good" come?

DM: That comes from seeing the historical performance of IPOs in the marketplace over the past number of years.

RL: Have you seen a fair number of IPOs that have tanked in their first 90 days?

DM: Oh yes! There have been quite a few. The best example right now is perhaps Dove Pharmaceuticals. That was a deal that originally came out of CIBC World Markets and broke its issue price and went down substantially because there were questions about whether or not the prospectus had given out all the important and relevant information that it should. From that point on, the issue was seen as damaged goods. Once a stock breaks its issue price, it has to climb a wall of worry on the part of investors; and as it gets back to its issue price there is generally a lot of supply from those investors with a horse racing mentality who are at that point just praying "Please, God, just let me get even!" But this is not the only one. There have been several others.

RL: Do you think that there is a regular issuance of shares by companies that are not really looking for cash to grow the company, but rather to cash out larger shareholders or to save the company from impending doom?

DM: I don't think that this happens very often at all. The disclosure requirements that are there today really promote the whole idea of caveat emptor [Let the buyer beware]. An investor should really look at a company that has a *firm-commitment* offering. We suggest that all of our investors follow that rule. You have private placement offerings, self-underwritten offerings, direct public offerings, and although they have the right to do these offerings, they are generally lower-quality offerings. Anything under the firm-commitment offering should be considered more risky than the firm commitment. I can't say that they are trying to squeak one by with a company that doesn't really need or deserve to go public, but the company is required to give adequate information for the investor to make an informed decision. If the investor does not do his or her own due diligence, therein lies the blame.

FIRM COMMITMENT: A firm commitment is a type of underwriting where the underwriters agree to buy the entire amount of the issue from the issuer. The underwriters act as a dealer and are responsible for any unsold inventory. They cannot return what they don't sell. The dealer profits from the spread between the purchase price and the public offering price.

RL: Are all IPOs created in essentially the same way?

DM: Yes, when an IPO is evolving. Investors must, however, realize that this is a multitiered process. A 5 million share IPO needs to have a minimum of 10 million shares that are subscribed to. That is necessary to sufficiently carry the stock past the initial offer. The underwriters must know that there is enough additional interest to provide buyers in the secondary market for those who simply flip the IPO. There must be enough interest in the stock to maintain a price that is above its issue price for a reasonable period of time. There has got to be a level of interest that will not only absorb sellers but also stimulate new buyers. Many smaller firms do not have the muscle to continue to get people to buy these shares. Smaller firms recognize this, which is why they often use a "best-efforts" approach to bringing a company public. They just don't have the manpower to keep up the momentum in the secondary market. In self-underwritten offerings and others it is just a matter of time before the stock begins to trend down under its offering price. The firm-commitment offering has the most support in the secondary market.

RL: Do you feel there is any great inefficiency in the IPO market?

DM: The inefficiencies exist in how the allocation process is met. I don't think anyone will ever legislate how a firm allocates shares to its investor clients. I am also not, however, a fan of the alternative referred to as a "Dutch auction" system that has been brought into the marketplace. Its design is such that the issuing company clearly benefits the most from the process. This is a result of the pricing being subject to the demand, which leaves investors open to pay the kinds of prices we saw in the late nineties without any solid valuation being set like you have in the firm-commitment offering. It is certainly a more economical way for a company to bring itself public, and it has the benefits of bringing in the potentially higher incremental dollars resulting from demand, but investors do not appear to be well rewarded. If it were a better deal for investors, this type of offering would have gained much more ground than it has. Though there is much more comprehensive information out there and access is aggregated and inexpensive through sites like www.ipofinancial.com, many people still rely on the marketing hype alone to influence their IPO investing decisions.

RL: What about interest in a particular issue. Is there anywhere to find out what issues are oversubscribed, etc.?

DM: Brokers often tell clients when issues appear to be oversubscribed; and though they are probably not doing anything illegal or unethical, this kind of information is not generally shared outside the syndicate members. And I imagine verifying this information real time would be almost impossible.

RL: What are the most common mistakes made by IPO investors?

DM: The emotionalism of IPO investing leaves many investors feeling that if they don't get the stock at the IPO price, they have missed the boat. The other thing is just playing IPOs and not playing the secondary offerings and other areas of the market. The third mistake and perhaps the most significant is not knowing the rules of the game. Those people often try to deal with a discount firm where they tell the broker that they want IPO stock without knowing how the game works.

RL: Do you have some specific recommendations for investors before putting their first dollar into the IPO market?

DM: First of all you have got to do your homework. You cannot rely on what a broker says, because in our business the brokers are generally not able to figure out whether a deal is going to work or not going to work. The broker may only have information that gives a short-term outlook on the company or the stock. The investors can very easily become the victim of the brokerage community. The broker asks the investors questions to qualify them, but rarely do the investors ask the broker questions about whether or not they should be doing business with the broker.

RL: What is the secret to actually getting shares of an IPO? It seems like the average investor only gets shares of offerings that he or she doesn't really want, while never being able to get shares of the hot IPOs.

DM: Just because a broker works for a firm bringing a company public does not mean that the broker can get IPO shares. When you are interviewing the broker, ask if he is regularly allocated IPO shares. If he says that he usually does not, but he will try for you, he is not the broker you want. If the broker says yes, but I have plenty of clients looking for IPOs, so I am not sure what I could get for you, then at least you have a chance. This broker may tell you outright that he allocates IPO shares to his best clients, which lets you know that you must either trade actively, invest heavily, or otherwise become a top-tier client to garner his favor. When a broker tells you he tried but couldn't get you any shares, he is lying. What he is really saying is that "I didn't really want to give you any of the IPO shares." It is still a quid pro quo environment. You must find out what the broker expects of you to get the shares you want. If the client will ask the hard questions and the broker is honest about what he expects the client to do to earn this business, then the relationship may grow. If the broker does not seemingly get IPO allocations or is just not willing to put them to you, then move on to another broker. This is about taking a big pat of butter and smoothing it out in all the right places.

RL: Can the broker offer any additional insights to an initial public offering that might help an investor to make an educated decision, or is the broker bound to speak only to what is detailed in the prospectus?

DM: The broker is bound by the prospectus. The broker can discuss the details of the offering and the company as it is reflected in the printed prospectus, and that is it.

RL: Are there any specific criteria to identify great IPOs?

DM: Well, depending on market conditions, the first thing people must understand is what the company does. If the investors do not understand what the IPO is about and what the company is about, they have relegated this important piece of the decision-making process to someone else who likely does not share their perspectives. Understanding what the company does and the purpose for the IPO is essential. The investor should see that the management is the best that they can get for the prospectus. They need to look at the financials of the company, including the footnotes, to find out why the company has turned in the results that it has. And then something that is oftentimes boring and seemingly boilerplate is the review of all the risk factors. That has to be done prior to the management's discussion of what the management says are the risk factors of the company. [This will prevent a tainted view and will sometimes bring about questions that may or may not be addressed elsewhere in the prospectus or management review.] It really depends on each company, product, and management, but every possible scenario should be considered.

RL: Are there any investors who you think should just stay away from IPOs?

DM: Yes, the investor who is looking to buy the company stock for long-term capital gains should not spend sleepless nights worrying about getting the IPO. Good stocks will hold up after the offering and should continue to move up over time.

IPO OPPORTUNITIES NOW

So where are the next opportunities and how can we find out which ones are going to be great and which ones are going to fizzle? Remember that as the world grows in population and technology, it actually moves us closer together. Though some financial theorists suggest that as one market falters, another one flies, this is most definitely not a rule to invest by. We have now seen instances where the major world powers either concurrently or in series undergo a period of recession. This may, in part, be due to the close correlation that major economies share with one another, or it may just be an anomaly. In any case, each market must be looked at independently as well as on a global perspective.

In emerging Asian and European markets, initial public offerings, secondary offerings, and even debt offerings are popping up all over with tremendous upside potential. *A note of caution in investing in foreign-based IPOs*: The regulatory and oversight authorities in other countries do not necessarily follow or enforce the same guidelines as those in the highly regulated United States. Proper due diligence and discovery measures should be taken with every issue.

In the United States, where more colleges offer degrees in entrepreneurship than in all other universities around the world combined, you can always find a great new business looking for funding. As the economy stabilizes, IPOs will start coming to market again. Don't wait for them to come to you. Look for areas in need and for products that might fill those needs. In the United States over the next decade, I am personally looking for the companies addressing issues associated with energy and, perhaps ironically, financial firms that offer absolute-return-focused funds and separately managed account programs.

And it is not just the IPO market that is going to grow over the next decade. The private-placement universe is finding more structure than it has in the past. Throughout Asia, the Pacific Rim, Europe, and the former Soviet Union new industry, manufacturing, and technology plays are emerging in a whirlwind of government reforms and new-found capitalist ideals.

The progenies of such massive paradigm shifts are new businesses. These businesses carry with them opportunity for investors that can only be garnered in times of dramatic and favorable economic change. For at least the next two decades we should find that such winds of change create long-lasting economic benefits on the order of those from the leaps in industrial growth seen in America around the turn of the twentieth century.

When we look at the wealth amassed by astute investors during that period, much of what we have seen in our most recent technological revolution still pales in comparison. Admittedly the Carnegies, the Rockefellers, the Morgans, and the Astors were not subject to the same income, property, estate, and gift taxes that we enjoy today, but the fundamentals of change were quite similar. Countries with a strengthening economic base, developing industrial infrastructure, and rapidly improving technology generally (not a mandate, but a guide) encounter a period of sustained market growth.

Something is going on somewhere right now, and if you feel like you missed the first wave of opportunity, be patient. It doesn't just happen once; and it is not like the mumps, where one occurrence is an inoculation against further outbreak. As a matter of fact, history shows that quite the opposite is true. Once a country begins down the path of revolutionary change, the momentum created increases the propensity for additional occurrences. Countries evolve much like children in that they are able to build on the knowledge and strengths of the past, and major events are woven into the core fabric, the psyche. Studies of the Dow have shown that oftentimes great market gains come after great market losses and vice versa. Many of the countries that went through a recession in the 1990s are now primed for new and accelerated growth.

As mentioned earlier, IPOs are not necessarily the lifeblood of emerging or growing markets, but they are, without a doubt, one of the metrics that illustrate the robustness of a particular market. IPOs aren't easy money, but there is a lot of money to be made when we do the work and know the game.

8

Options Are
for Risk Takers

W hen options began trading on the CBOE (Chicago Board Options Exchange) in 1973, contract volume was dominated by hedgers and speculators. Since the early 1980s, option volume has grown from less than 8 million contracts per month to more than 1 million contracts per day. In addition to the equity and index options traded at the CBOE, options are also traded at the American Stock Exchange, Pacific Exchange, and Philadelphia Stock Exchange. As a result of the increased volume and competition, the emergence of a new electronic platform called the International Securities Exchange, or ISE, was launched in 2000. This new electronic exchange intensified competition by reducing exchange fees, narrowing the spread between the bid and ask, and offering independent quote dissemination for multiple market makers. All these changes improve efficiencies and reduce costs, which directly benefits both the investor and the trader.

As in any area of investing, most options investors and traders have heard the stories of great riches being made and of great fortunes being lost—probably because some of both are indeed true. Prudent investors would be well served to invest the time to establish a base of knowledge in the area of option investing. There is so much value in having options in and on your portfolio that I will certainly not be able to do them justice in one short chapter. Options are like insurance. They can protect your portfolio and help you sleep at night, but if you don't know the difference between "whole life" and "term," you may be paying for something you don't need, and in turn, you may get less than you deserve.

An option is a marvelous resource both for leverage and for insurance. We will discuss the merits and concerns of both. The danger with leverage is that those who are simply speculating without the proper training or risk controls are susceptible to losing their money faster. But this is nothing new; and it exists in every marketplace. Anyone jumping into volatile sectors of the stock market without a plan may get crushed just as quickly.

THE OPTION COWBOY

The argument against options has generally come from those who are either completely unfamiliar with the concept, uneducated in regard to the simplest and most effective strategies, or competing for business in another market. Clients who are trading options without a solid understanding of the options market often exacerbate this concern. It doesn't take years of schooling to make options an extremely valuable arrow in your investing quiver. If there is no active risk management by the broker or the investor, and if the intent is simply to gain leverage on an already high-risk investment, there is cause to associate the action with gambling. In the practice of law we weigh penalties and judgments oftentimes on the intent of the offender. Investing and trading can be similarly appraised, as you may find some people who are gambling side by side with other people who are clearly investing. What separates them is their intent. Financial markets, like thousands of other markets, do create an opportunity for those with a penchant for gambling, but the fundamental differences between the financial options markets and gambling are numerous.

The options market in and of itself has no inherent ties to any structured game of chance. In fact, I would argue that the option is extremely underutilized by today's investors.

Before getting into the specifics of how and why options are beneficial in securing the smooth and long-term performance of your portfolio, we will review the basic building blocks of the options market. There are two primary options in the financial markets: The call option and the put option.

THE CALL OPTION

A call option is a contract that gives the purchaser the right (but not the obligation) to buy, or "call," a particular stock or commodity at a specific price for a predetermined period of time. *For example*: An investor who, in January, purchases a Dell March 50 call will have the ability to purchase the stock at $50 per share until the expiration of the contract on the third Friday of March. Should Dell rise at or before the expiration date, the purchaser of the call would be able to exercise the option and purchase the shares at 50. The seller, or "writer," of the call option would be obligated to deliver the shares at the prearranged, or "strike," price of $50 per share. If the stock were presently trading at $60 per share, the purchaser would see a profit equal to $10 per share (the amount above the strike price that the stock is trading at exercise) times 100 shares (each equity option is for 100 shares of the underlying stock) minus the premium paid for the option.

The purchase of a call option is generally done in expectation of a rise in the price of the underlying.

THE PUT OPTION

A put option is a contract that gives the purchaser the right (but not the obligation) to sell, or "put," a particular stock or commodity at a specific price for a predetermined period of time. *For example*: An investor who, in April, purchases a Dell June 50 put option will have the ability to sell the stock at $50 per share until the expiration of the contract on the third Friday of June. Should Dell fall at or before the expiration date, the purchaser of the put would be able to exercise the option and sell the shares at 50. The seller, or writer, of the put option would be obligated to buy the shares at the prearranged, or strike, price of $50 per share. If the stock were presently trading at $40 per share, the purchaser would see a profit equal to $10 per share (the amount below the strike price that the stock is trading at exercise) times 100 shares (each equity option is for 100 shares of the underlying stock) minus the premium paid for the option.

The purchase of a put option is generally done in expectation of a fall in the price of the underlying.

WHAT'S BEHIND AN OPTION

The comparison I like to use for describing stock options is real estate. When I was living in south Florida, it was not terribly uncommon to hear of someone offering up a private beachfront home with the idea that a commercial buyer would either move the home or tear it down to make room for some new high-rise condominium development or hotel. An astute real estate investor, on hearing of such news, would likely approach the seller and ask for an option on the property. The option would be for a specific price, say $500,000, and for a specific period of time, say three months. The seller would ask that the investor pay a premium of some sort for holding the property. A 1 percent premium for such an option would be $5000. The investor would then begin working with her contacts in the property development world to find some interest. If the investor were able to locate and contract with another purchaser, she would stand to net the difference between the strike price of $500,000 and the selling price. If the property developer's acquaintances were to agree to a purchase price of $800,000, the investor who purchased the option would stand to gain $295,000 ($800,000 − $500,000 − $5000). Not too bad a return on a $5000 investment. Were the investor only able to find someone willing to pay $500,000, she would not make enough to pay for the $5000 spent on the purchase of the option. The option agreement made between the property seller and the investor is the same as a call option in the stock and commodity markets. The investor paid a premium to the property seller to lock in a purchase price for a specific amount of time. You could say she put the property on layaway for a small fee. An investor who buys a call option is acquiring the same right. Where the option in the real estate example is on land, the option in the stock market is on a specific financial instrument. In either case, the entity on which the option is created is called the *underlying*.

OPTION PRICING

An options contract integrates the value of the underlying stock or commodity with an added premium for the risk associated with the potential movement over time of the stock price against the seller of the contract. The premium (or fee) is broken down into two parts: The amount charged for the *intrinsic value* of the option and the amount charged for the *time value*. The intrinsic value is simply the value that the option has because of its strike price in relationship to the present price of the underlying (stock, commodity, real estate, etc.). The following influence the price of an option:

1. Strike price
2. Time to expiration
3. Volatility
4. Interest rates
5. Supply and demand

Strike price

If a call option on IBM with a strike price of 60 ($60 per share) is trading at $2[*] and IBM is only trading at $56 per share, there is no intrinsic value to the option. The stock must rise in price before the option has real intrinsic value. The entire premium in this example comes from time value and is paid for the risk assumed by the seller (or writer) of the option. Options with different strike prices include OTMs, ATMs, and ITMs:

OTM. An out-of-the-money option is one that has a strike price that, in the case of a call option, is higher than the actual price of the stock or commodity. In the case of a put, the strike price is below the actual price of the stock or commodity. An out-of-the-money option has only time value. It has no intrinsic value.

ATM. An at-the-money option has a strike price at or near the actual price of the stock or commodity. An at-the-money option has little or no intrinsic value but like all options has time value until expiration.

ITM. An in-the-money option has a strike price that, in the case of a call option, is lower than the actual price of the stock or commodity. In the case of a put, the strike price is above the actual price of the stock or commodity. An in-the-money option has both intrinsic and time value. A call with a $50 strike price on a stock trading at 55 has $5 dollars in intrinsic value per share ($55 − $50 = $5). A put with a $50 strike price on a stock trading at 45 also has $5 in intrinsic value per share ($50 − $45 = $5). (See Exhibit 8–1.)

---

[*]With stocks, each options contract is quoted per share, but each contract is actually for 100 shares; so the actual premium paid is 100 times the quoted price. In this case the premium would be $200.

Options Screen

Calls Symbol	Last	Change	Bid	Ask	Volume	Open Int	Strike Price
DLYFD.X	14.7	0	15.3	15.4	0	33	20
DLQFX.X	13.1	0	12.8	12.9	0	3	22.5
DLQFE.X	9.5	0	10.3	10.4	0	62	25
DLQFY.X	6.9	0	7.8	7.9	0	420	27.5
DLQFF.X	5.5↑	0.9	5.3	5.5	112	1,222	30
DLQFZ.X	3↑	0.7	2.9	3	699	4,927	32.5
DLQFG.X	0.9↑	0.3	0.85	0.95	10,217	18,810	35
DLQFT.X	0.1↑	0.05	0.05	0.1	229	22,380	37.5
DLQFH.X	0.05	0	N/A	0.05	55	2,901	40
DLQFS.X	0	0	N/A	0.05	0	0	42.5
DLQFI.X	0.05	0	N/A	0.05	0	19	45

Highlighted options are in-the-money.

EXHIBIT 8-1 **Options Expiring Fri, Jun 18, 2004**

Time to Expiration

Time is money ... and opportunity ... and risk. For the buyer of an option, time is a friend, but for the seller, it is a liability. The further out an option expiration date, the higher the relative premium. The seller has a higher risk whether it is real or perceived.

What kind of risk does the seller (or writer) of the option take? In the case of a call option, the writer or seller of the option is guaranteeing delivery of the underlying at the strike price. In theory, the writer of the call has unlimited risk, because, in theory, the stock could go to infinity. In writing put options the risk is limited to the strike price times the number of shares, because the maximum risk for the writer is that the stock goes to zero. This risk grows in significance with the amount of time remaining until expiration.

As a buyer of an option, you would prefer to have the most time possible for the underlying stock to move in your favor. Time is a good thing for the buyer. As a seller of an option, you would prefer to have only minimal

Puts Symbol	Last	Change	Bid	Ask	Volume	Open Int
DLYRD.X	0	0	N/A	0.05	0	0
DLQRX.X	0	0	N/A	0.05	0	0
DLQRE.X	0.05	0	N/A	0.05	0	15
DLQRY.X	0.05	0	N/A	0.05	0	22
DLQRF.X	0.05	0	N/A	0.05	10	942
DLQRZ.X	0.1 ↓	0.1	0.05	0.1	635	8,739
DLQRG.X	0.55 ↓	0.45	0.5	0.6	996	15,629
DLQRT.X	2.25 ↓	0.75	2.2	2.3	1,137	5,541
DLQRH.X	5.2	0	4.6	4.7	0	51
DLQRS.X	8	0	7.1	7.2	0	220
DLQRI.X	10.4	0	9.6	9.7	60	40

time for the underlying stock to move against you. Though a seller (writer) of an option takes in premium dollars at the time of the sale, the liability associated with the sale is not gone until the exercise or expiration of the contract. A writer of an options contract has the potential for losing the dollars acquired from the sale and more. When options are used in an organized fashion, the risk can be easily kept in check.

Exhibit 8–2 depicts the loss in value from an option due to time decay alone. As a buyer of an option, time eats away at gains, while the seller of an option benefits from the same effect.

Volatility

The degree to which the price of a stock or commodity moves over time will define its volatility. Securities with higher volatilities will command higher premiums, whereas those with lower volatilities will tend to carry lower relative premiums, with all other factors being the same.

Theoretical Call Option Time Premium Decay

EXHIBIT 8-2   Stock=$50; Strike=$50; Volatility=30%; Int. Rate=6%; No Dividends.
(Courtesy of The Options Industry Council)

Volatility may be one of the most critical components in the pricing of an option. Dozens of books and hundreds of trading systems have been written with option volatility as the subject. Where some fear large price swings, others find favor in them. Mastering the basic principles of option volatility can supercharge your investing.

Exhibit 8–3 shows two equities that went up approximately the same amount over the same period of time but experienced very different volatility. Though the two stocks are in the same industry and the same sector, the variation in the range of price for security BBH (upper chart) makes it more volatile. Consequently the premium would likely be higher for this security.

Interest Rates

Option premiums react inversely to interest rates. When interest rates are rising, potential option buyers weigh the potential return of the investment in an option against the potential returns in other investment vehicles. When alternative investments become more attractive, option buyers go in other directions, and premiums naturally decline. In contrast, when interest rates fall, options have a tendency to become more desirable, and premiums increase as a result.

BBH-DNA Percent Comparison

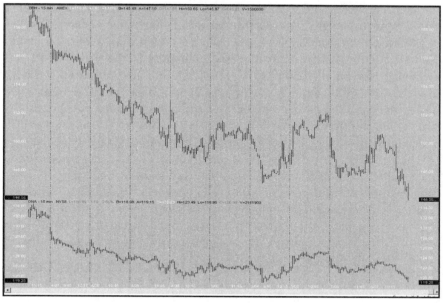

EXHIBIT 8-3

Supply and Demand

In addition to interest rates, other factors can affect the supply and demand for options. When there is fear of coming volatility, option sellers are less likely to offer many contracts at each strike price, and the limited offering pushes premiums higher. In rapidly changing or trending markets, supply runs lighter since there is less confidence in direction. Even in trending markets, premiums may remain high if sellers are uncertain of market momentum over time. In consolidating markets more sellers come to market to take advantage of the natural stability, which drives premium down.

POWER UP YOUR PORTFOLIO

Rather than an extended discourse on the literally dozens of uses for options in a conservative portfolio, three concrete examples may be of greater service.

This is by no means meant to be a training manual for trading options, nor is it intended to promote any specific trades or trading styles. We have all seen the disclosure "Past performance is no guarantee of future results" in advertisements for financial products. But we all want to know past performance, as it is still one of the best indicators we have for future performance even if it is reasonable to expect that future performance will most likely differ. Option strategies are no exception. In certain time frames and with certain equities and commodities, the risk to reward is substantially better than in other strategies. It is imperative that you perform due diligence on each strategy depending on your portfolio and the goals you have for the portfolio. This means reviewing the number of contracts traded to make sure there is adequate interest on the other side of the trade. It means knowing how the option itself responds in both sedate and volatile markets. It also means measuring the upside and downside potential. Once you have used a certain strategy for a while, you will gain a sense of comfort. Never let comfort replace research. Do your homework. It is always time well spent. Here are three of my favorites:

1. The Covered Call: Adding Portfolio Income While Reducing Risk

As noted earlier, a call is an option giving the buyer the right but not the obligation to purchase a security at a particular price for a specified period of time. In a covered call strategy you are writing or selling the call option for the purpose of bringing in premium.

FEATURES

Selling a call option when you don't own the underlying security is called *naked call writing* for reasons that should be obvious. If the price of the underlying stock or commodity goes higher than the strike price of the option sold, you will be required to go into the market and buy the security to make good on the delivery promised through the writing (selling) of the option.

With a covered call you are selling an option that gives the purchaser a right to buy the security that you already own at a preset price.

EXAMPLE

- You purchase 100 shares of XYZ at $50 per share for a total investment of $5000.

- You sell (write) a call that expires in three months (a covered call, because you own the stock) at a strike price of $55 for $2 in premium.
- The income from the sale of the covered call is $200 (options are quoted per share, but each contract represents 100 shares).

POSSIBLE OUTCOMES

SCENARIO 1. The stock drops $5, or 10 percent, over the course of the quarter (the contract period), and the option expires worthless.

Results: Since $200 was taken in from the covered call, the net loss is only $300 rather than $500. This is a 40 percent reduction in risk.

SCENARIO 2. The stock rises $5, or 10 percent, over the course of the quarter, and the option, written with a strike price of $55 still expires worthless.

Results: Since $200 was taken in from the sale of the covered call, the net gain is actually $700 ($500 from the rise in price + $200 in call premium). This is a 40 percent increase in the net profitability from the position.

SCENARIO 3. The stock surges $10 per share or 20 percent, over the course of the contract period and is exercised.

Results: The purchaser of the call option is sold your 100 shares (the stock is "called away") of XYZ for $55 per share (the strike price of the options contract), giving you $5 per share profit from the original purchase. You also keep the premium amount of $200, or $2 per share, for a net gain of $700. Though the profitability is no less than in scenario 2, having just held the stock without the call writing would have yielded a profit of $1000 under this scenario.

IMPORTANT NOTES

- When stocks have large moves like this, the profits can be capped, leaving the investor with less than optimal performance.
- A prudent covered-call writing strategy can yield premiums like those in the example four or more times per year. For longer-term investments the premiums should more than make up for those instances where the stock is called away.
- If XYZ remained at or near $50 per share for the entire year, covered-call writing could realistically return $8 per share, or *an additional 16 percent return.*

2. The Married Put: Defining Risk with Insurance for Your Portfolio

For those of you who are married, this technique is easy to remember, because most of us reviewed our life insurance needs once we expanded our family. If your stock portfolio is a substantial part of your net worth or your retirement planning, you should research in detail how puts may save your portfolio from devastation. A married put simply involves the purchase of a put option on stock that you own.

FEATURES

This option will enable you to sell your stock at the strike price regardless of how far it might have fallen over the contract period. It essentially guarantees a limit to the losses you might incur should your stock take a terrible tumble.

EXAMPLE
- You purchased 100 shares of ZYX at $25 per share one year ago for a total investment of $2500.
- Your 100-share investment is now worth $5000.
- Long term the stock continues to look good, but increasing volatility in the markets has you concerned. You decide that you are willing to take some pain, maybe 20 percent ($10 per share), but you don't want to give back everything you have made.
- You purchase a put with a strike price of $40 that does not expire for six months for 80 cents ($0.80 × 100 = $80).

POSSIBLE OUTCOMES

SCENARIO 1. ZYX stock drops $5 over the six-month period, which is not enough to warrant the put option. Your portfolio remains in an area you have deemed safe, but you have spent $80 on insurance, adding slightly to your loss.

SCENARIO 2. ZYX stock drops back to your original purchase price of $25 per share, but your put option limits the loss to $10 instead of $25. The total loss now looks like this: Loss in stock value (−$25) + gain in put option value ($15) − premium paid for option ($0.80) = −$10.80 per share. In this case the loss has been limited to 21.6 percent rather than 50 percent.

SCENARIO 3. The ZYX stock you own soars to $70 per share, and the put option expires worthless. Your stock increases by another $20 per share, or 40 percent, minus the $0.80 spent on the married put.

IMPORTANT NOTES

Insurance is never fun to buy, but it will promote the stability of your entire portfolio. This is the ounce of prevention that can eliminate the need for a pound of cure. An important thing to remember when using a married put is to treat it like life or health insurance. It is just portfolio insurance. In that light, pay as little as you can to get the coverage you need. If you own ZYX at $50 per share, is it really worth buying puts with a strike price at 50, or do you really only need to be insured if it drops below 40 or 45? You decide. The closer the put is to the actual price of the stock, the more expensive it will be.

If paying for this kind of insurance gets under your skin, consider a third option.

3. The Collar: Have Your Cake and Eat It Too

This is a combination of strategies 1 and 2. It is a great concept for the conservative investor. A collar uses some of the premium brought in from covered-call writing to purchase the married put.

FEATURES

Because the premium is often larger for the sale of the call, the investor can buy a put that is "closer to the money" (to the present stock price) or just keep the extra cash.

If the point in collaring the trade is strictly to pay for the insurance (put buying), then the call writing should be done as far out-of-the-money as possible.

IMPORTANT NOTES

Since many people selling covered calls prefer selling the nearest expiration date (within three months or less) and buying puts that have more time to expiration, two things happen: (1) The difference between the dollars earned for the sale of the call and the dollars paid for the put is narrowed. (2) The time value garnered in the covered-call writing is comparatively smaller than that of the longer-term put purchased.

There may be only two puts purchased per year, but there may be four call options sold during the same period. This approach is very useful in adding income and providing protection for investors who hold or intend to hold positions for years.

Collars are extremely handy in situations where large gains have been made and where there is presently no fundamental or technical reason for selling. Instead of the old trader's adage of "When in doubt, get out!" you can lock in profits and maintain a vantage point for seeing new gains.

None of these strategies are difficult to learn. They can save the life of your portfolio, and they can add double-digit returns to your performance. When you listen closely, you will find that those who rant and rave about the dangers of options have little or no knowledge of options. Others have been hurt in the options market because they never took the time to attend a class or study options. Why jump into any worthwhile endeavor without study. The study is what brings confidence and enjoyment to the pursuit.

C H A P T E R

Diversification Eliminates Risk

The mantra of diversification has been well intended but terribly misguided. Brokers and investment advisers find it easy to sell the concept of diversification to clients. Diversification sounds good, and it seems to make sense, but Wall Street has all but forgotten the principles. The concept of diversification centers on the idea that different groups of stocks perform well over time, and if you are vested across a broad selection of these stocks, the chance for any one stock or fund to hurt your portfolio is lessened. In theory, there is also a higher likelihood of being in the right investment when it moves. For many, that is about as far as the thought process goes. In reality, much more is involved in proper diversification.

A typical portfolio may look something like this:

25%	Aggressive growth
20%	Blue chip
20%	Value
15%	International
10%	Index fund
10%	Bond fund

The benefits to this diversified portfolio seem to be:

1. It covers a wide array of market sectors and so could benefit from any of them going up in value.

2. If any one area is crushed, the impact will be dispersed across the weight of the portfolio.

3. If there is a global bull market, all the sectors should fare well, except maybe the bond fund.

The drawbacks to this diversified portfolio may include:

1. Should any individual area excel, the positive impact will be diffused, and the portfolio will rarely benefit from exceptional returns.

2. If there is a global bear market, this long-only portfolio will be sunk, with only a small percentage in bonds left to keep it afloat.

3. When the bonds are profitable, it is generally accepted that some or all of the equity groups will be underperforming. Furthermore, it is unlikely that at any one time all of the investments will be bringing positive absolute net returns to the table.

4. There is often little consideration for active risk management in a portfolio "protected" by diversification.

5. There is little guarantee that the correlation between the different groups has stayed the same since the portfolio began. Rebalancing portfolios according to sectors does not reduce risk if the sectors are highly correlated.

6. There is no diversification across time. Expectations are that markets will always trend up, and over time diversified portfolios will capture the breadth of the global marketplace.

7. There is no diversification of strategies. The strategy is the same for each area: buy and hold.

So how diversified is your portfolio? Probably not as diversified as you think, or want. As more and more mutual funds have appeared, the lines between growth and value have blurred. When dissecting portfolios, you can expect to find many of the same stocks showing up in multiple funds. Companies like Cisco Systems (CSCO), a manufacturer of routers and servers, is consistently seen in select hardware funds, Internet funds, technology funds, value funds, and growth funds. I can see how Cisco could be justified as a holding for any one of these funds, but it doesn't keep us well diversified.

In contrast, most of the large funds hold 120 to 150 names in their portfolio at any given point. This raises a question of practicality, or at least one of feasibility. Doesn't it seem a bit zealous to expect any manager to efficiently monitor the news on each company and its peers as well as production, sales, earnings, margins, and more? Moreover, the opportunity for a fund manager to significantly and consistently outperform the market indexes should diminish as the fund grows in number and more closely resembles the actual index it is trying to beat.

These are problems of *overdiversification.* As a rule I try not to invest in the largest mutual funds for this reason alone.

INTERNATIONAL DIVERSIFICATION

The last two decades of the twentieth century brought the investing world closer together than it has ever been. Economies of Europe, Asia, and Latin America are now closely tied to that of the United States. When the primary markets of the United States move sharply in one direction, you can bet that the momentum will carry over into the foreign markets. It takes a bit of work to find those international investment funds that move independently of domestic funds.

A PARADIGM CHANGE

If you could change your investing paradigm to one where you could expect each investment to bring profits into the portfolio without regard to market direction or volatility, would you?

If you knew that every manager handling your account was being compensated based strictly upon the profits he or she earned, would you feel better about investing?

Would you sleep better knowing that if a war breaks out or a foreign bank fails, your managers will be excited about the opportunities rather than afraid of the consequences?

Could you imagine having investments that find profits in uptrends by buying stocks, profits in downtrends from shorting stocks, and profits in sideways markets from selling premium on options?

A strong portfolio should be diversified across profit centers rather than just market sectors. A truly diversified portfolio should consider more than just an asset class or sector. Consideration should be given to diversification across strategies as well as time horizons.

Markets are dynamic. They move up, down, and sideways. They move in cycles that sometimes last days or weeks and at other times last for months and even years. If the prudent investor truly seeks consistency over time, diversification should be modeled to reduce those factors that undermine either the consistency or proficiency of a portfolio. After all, this is really the goal we hope to achieve from our diversification model.

Martial arts legend Bruce Lee taught his students, "Empty your mind. Be formless, shapeless, like water. You put water into a cup it becomes the cup. Put it into a teapot it becomes the teapot. Now water can flow, or creep, or drip or crash. Be like water, my friend."

Remember the equity curve (see Exhibits 1–5a and b). Plotted on a chart measuring the performance of a particular security over time, it is a line or a curve representing the growth in the value of an investment in the security. A smooth equity curve reflects less performance volatility. The equity curve of your portfolio is simply a time line connecting the dots of monthly, quarterly, or yearly performance. An investment with profits of 5 percent in one quarter followed by losses of 3 percent the next quarter followed by profits of 8 percent the next quarter and losses of 6 percent the next quarter produces results that are almost identical to an investment that consistently earns 7/8 percent per quarter. The difference is the volatility and risk associated with the first investment as compared with the second. In this instance the returns may be similar, but the consistency of the second would yield a smoother equity curve.

This is not to say that your investing should always make money over every time period. It is to say, however, that a prudent mixture of strategies with varying time horizons will over time produce a much smoother equity curve than simple diversification across asset classes. The power in designing a great portfolio may begin with a traditional Asset Class Menu, like the one depicted in Exhibit 9–1, but the percentage allocations and associated requirements for a change in each allocation can vary immensely. Consequently, performances can be greatly varied as well.

Asset Class Menu

EQUITIES					
Domestic					**International**
VALUE			VALUE		
Large Cap	Mid Cap	Small Cap	Large Cap	Mid Cap	Small Cap
GROWTH			VALUE		
Large Cap	Mid Cap	Small Cap	Large Cap	Mid Cap	Small Cap

FIXED INCOME					
Domestic					**International**
HIGH QUALITY			HIGH YIELD		
Corporate	Mortage-backed	Government	Corporate	Mortage-backed	Government

OPTIONS					
Equity	Index	Commodity	Futures Currency		Foreign

FUTURES					
Equity	Index	Commodity	Bond Currency		Foreign

PRECIOUS METALS		
Gold	Silver	Platinum

REAL ESTATE				
Rental	Residential	Multiunit	Farm	Commercial

COLLECTIBLES				
Art	Antiques	Automobiles	Coins	Stamps

EXHIBIT 9-1

Considering the investment strategy, style, and time frame in addition to the asset class must be a vigilant effort made in a consistent manner to ensure performance quality. The fear and concern that accompany the buy-and-hold portfolio can be all but eradicated with these simple modifications.

The perfect portfolio should reflect the personal desires and goals of the owner. There is immense opportunity in long and short funds, short-term trading systems, convertible arbitrage models, emerging-market debt funds, distressed equity funds, and others. Build your own portfolio of alternative managers or get a professional to assist you. If you want to ensure the future of your portfolio, take charge of it. It is your money and your future.

Different managers find value in different styles, which can prove to be to everyone's good fortune. For example, let's look at three distinctly different long/short managers: The first manager, let's call her Alice, will use the market's general trend to determine her trading bias. If the market is moving steadily upward, Alice identifies stocks that over the next 6 to 18 months (medium term) should be part of or even lead this trend. If and when the market changes direction, Alice will begin looking for stocks that may have been overlooked fundamentally and technically to sell short. She will begin selling the long positions that break down fundamentally or technically. In sideways markets, Alice will tend to maintain an even split between her long and short positions.

Steve is also a long/short manager, but his style is shorter term, as he holds positions in the portfolio for three weeks to three months on average. In addition to looking at equities over a shorter time frame, Steve employs a sector-rotation model whereby he looks at groups of similar stocks or sectors together rather than individually. His understanding of institutional order flow makes him keenly aware of which sectors the large institutions are buying and which sectors they are selling. Steve combines this knowledge with his fundamental and technical analysis to identify sectors trending up and sectors trending down.

Mark is another long/short manager specializing in statistical arbitrage. Mark also looks at sectors, but he sees each sector as a school of fish. He monitors the school of fish for divergence. Any number of things can cause the school (the group of stocks) to move closer together or to widen apart: news, earnings reports, government reports, and market volatility are but a sampling. The philosophy behind Mark's statistical arbitrage model is that the school may spread apart, but it generally comes back together. The risk management put in place is to ensure that the occasional stock eaten by a shark is not expected to rejoin the group (read Enron et al.). Profit is made by selling short the stock or stocks that have most accelerated and buying or going long the stock or stocks that have not moved significantly or have moved in the opposite direction. In Exhibit 9–2, we see can see how Wal-Mart (WMT) and Target (TGT) move together. Wal-Mart is the stock at the top of the chart, and Target (TGT) is the stock at the bottom of the chart.

Whether the price of Wal-Mart comes down or the price of Target goes up is not important. What is important is that the difference or spread between the two narrows. Two sample trades are shown in Exhibit 9–2 and the results are presented in Exhibit 9-3.

The goal in this strategy is to put on the trade while the related companies' stock prices have diverged, with the expectation of closing the trade once the spread has converged. In Exhibit 9–3, the column entitled "Change in Spread" reflects the profit per share traded. In the first trade, 100 shares of Wal-Mart are sold short, and 100 shares of Target are bought, with a dif-

WMT, TGT Two Trades

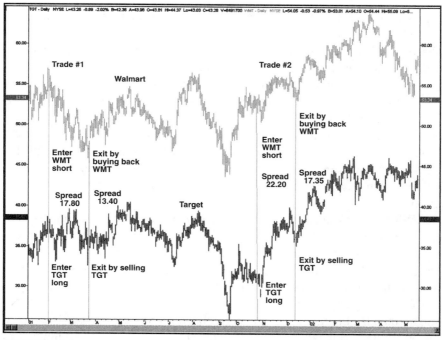

EXHIBIT 9-2

Wal-Mart–Target Spread

| Pair: | Trade 1 | | | Trade 2 | | |
| | Enter | Exit | | Enter | Exit | |
	1-Feb	27-Mar	Change in Spread	24-Sep	13-Dec	Change in Spread
Wal-Mart	$55.70	$50.30	$5.40	$53.30	$53.36	($0.06)
Target	$37.90	$36.90	($1.00)	$31.10	$36.01	$4.91
SPREAD	$17.80	$13.40	$4.00	$22.20	$17.35	$4.85
Profit on 100 shrs			$400.00			$485.00

EXHIBIT 9-3

ference between the two stock prices (the spread) being $17.80. Once the spread narrowed to $13.40, the positions were closed and a profit of $4 per share, or $400, is realized. The second trade is done in a similar fashion, with the total change in spread improving by $4.85 per share.

Take, for example, three managers all considered to be long/short managers, but with distinct contrasts in style and time horizons. Because of this heterogeneity, their performance will have little correlation to one another. Equally important is the absolute-return focus for each of these investment models. None are dependent upon the market going up to realize a profit. The same results can be acquired in all stock classes, including growth, value, international, emerging markets, and even real estate. It is a different paradigm.

When I speak to groups about comparing the old diversification logic to this more useful one, I can't help but think about the movie character Crocodile Dundee. In the first movie, Crocodile Dundee was taking one of his first strolls through New York City after spending his entire life in Australia's wild and woolly outback. A mugger came up to Dundee and drew a knife with a blade standing about 6 inches, and put it in front of the Aussie's face. No sooner than the mugger had made his demand for money, Dundee had drawn his own knife, which was easily twice the size. His reply to the mugger was "*That's* not a knife. *This* is a knife." Well my friends, *this* is diversification.

Each manager excels in his and her own right by keeping focused on a specific area of the market. This focus brings about returns that would be more difficult to find through the broad-based mutual fund investing. More importantly, risk is well defined and easy to manage due to the limited securities involved and the technical analysis employed. While investors may find comfort in following the cautionary words of Miguel de Cervantes "It is the part of a wise man . . . not to venture all of his eggs in one basket," by maintaining only portions of a portfolio in a single investment, money managers are proved to fare better when they adhere to the wisdom of Mark Twain, who said, "Put all your eggs in one basket and—watch that basket."

DOING ONE JOB RIGHT

I can't list the multitude of great trader's and money managers who have amassed fortunes through their focus on specific markets, or even specific areas of an individual market. One example would be Dave Floyd.

Dave Floyd, managing member of Aspen Trading, is located in Ben, Oregon, but his expertise has taken him around the world. He has garnered international recognition for his trading skills, and if you frequent TradingMarkets.com, you have no doubt seen one of his regular commentaries. Every time that I speak with Dave, I am impressed with his humble nature. What may be fascinating to those who believe that the more diversification the better is that Dave Floyd actually reduces his risk by focusing only on a limited group of investments during any given time period. In the following pages, Dave shares a perspective that has worked in the bond market, the equity markets, and now the foreign currency markets.

RL: When did you begin trading completely on your own?

DF: I left working on a bond desk around 1994 to trade directly in the equity markets. While I was active in the bond market in the very early nineties, I couldn't help but notice all of the action in equities. I was trading some in the equity markets prior to leaving the desk and finding great opportunity. So when I took the step to go out on my own, I chose the equity markets.

RL: So you went where the action was? I assume that is because action and volatility present opportunity?

DF: Exactly.

RL: Since the early nineties did you ever move into other markets? Did you venture back into bonds or options?

DF: Actually, I think much of my success may be due to my focus. For 10 years the equity markets provided a great resource for my trading style. The methods that I use do best when I can consistently find limited-risk high-reward trading opportunities. Though the equity markets have slowed considerably in the past few years, they still offer opportunity to the disciplined trader or investor. There may not be as much there now as there was before, but there is still money to be made.

Strategy

RL: Over the past couple of years you have begun to incorporate foreign currency or Forex trading into your repertoire. Why is that?

DF: The Forex market has a lot of the same great action now that the equity markets had in the nineties. There is plenty of movement, and plenty of liquidity, which makes for great trading. That being said, I still trade a select group of stocks every day as well.

RL: I understand that you became successful in the Forex markets quite rapidly. Were you able to incorporate the same strategies that you use in the equity markets?

DF: My primary strategy has always remained the same. It works in most any market where there is active movement. There are always nuances associated with each market that must be learned, but the basics remain the same.

RL: How complex is your primary strategy?

DF: It is actually very simple. Being simple is what makes it effective in so many markets. I follow the trend. Whether investing for months at a time or making trades that last only minutes, I always, always go in the direction of the trend. This reduces the likelihood of big moves against my position, and with all other things remaining the same, my position will continue in the same general direction.

RL: Do you ever include breakouts, or countertrends, or any other methods in your trading or investing?

DF: Very rarely. There is no reason to add spice to something that already tastes great. The markets provide enough profits for me without the extra headache. I keep it simple. When markets run up, I look to buy them once they have let off a little steam and pulled back. I enter my positions as they turn to move back in the direction of the general trend. There are some techniques for doing this with increased efficiency and effectiveness, but the basic concept is just that simple.

Those times where I do buy for a breakout are when I buy in anticipation of a breakout through a resistance level where support is nearby. This way, I have very little downside risk, and great upside potential if the breakout occurs. But the relative amount of risk I take is never increased to fit a trade. The trade has to fit my risk parameters.

Some people wait for the action to take place before they get in a position. In my opinion the support levels in those kinds of trades are just too far away, and so the risk is typically not acceptable to me. My trading style is characterized by shorter-term trading. Even my investments are shorter than most people's, because I require my positions to remain in a favorable trend.

RL: Have you focused your efforts in certain areas of the markets, and what changes that focus?

DF: I tend to stick to large-cap stocks typically traded on the NYSE. In the currency markets I trade the majors. On any given day I am looking at what I watched the previous day while making small changes to account for news or changes in the volatility of the sectors that I am watching or trading.

RL: Do you find that particular stocks or sectors rotate in and out of favor.

DF: Absolutely. Some sectors will trend for a few days or a week, while others trend for months. By actively trading or investing in those sectors with strong trends, I am able to capture the best of what the market has to offer. I stay in those sectors until they quit trending. If they begin trending in the other direction, I just trade in the direction of the new trend. If they start going sideways, I move on to something trending.

RL: So you don't really change your style to meet changing markets? You just find stocks (or currencies) that fit your style?

DF: Exactly.

Foreign Currency Markets

RL: What is it about the currency markets that make them so attractive?

DF: Well, there are a few things. First they are the largest markets in the world, which means that problems with liquidity are almost unheard of. Second, they trade 24 hours a day, which makes them great for trading when the rest of the markets are closed or just flat. The third thing is that they trade in trends for longer periods of time, which gives me something to do in addition to my equity trading that doesn't require such close attention. It is a perfect market for someone who doesn't want to trade extremely short term.

RL: Liquidity has become something of a problem in recent years in the equity markets. Why is that important?

DF: I can only buy so much of a gold stock or biotech without moving the price up. I have the same problem when trying to sell. In the foreign currency markets, the strategy that I use for one lot works exactly the same with fifty lots.

RL: How do Forex markets trend differently than equity markets trend?

DF: Because there are so many players, they move smoothly, and they trade with great technical precision. Intraday swings can be large, but the swings are easy to follow as a technical trader. The Forex markets may be the purest markets in existence.

RL: What do you mean by "purest market"?

DF: They just trade so technically, and they trade as a network rather than through an exchange. Where you are often at the mercy of the specialist with your order on an exchange like the NYSE, in the foreign currency markets what you see is what you get. It may be that everyone uses very similar technical analysis techniques and that this results in a kind of self-fulfilling prophecy.

Diversification

RL: While most people have learned that the safest investing involves staying diversified, you say that you are taking less risk while your positions tend to be heavily concentrated in only a few sectors.

DF: My risk is well defined for each position. That is how I have been able to maintain the integrity of my performance. By limiting my risk per trade and by actively putting my dollars where the strongest trends are, I am always, by virtue of my methodology, exactly where I want to be.

RL: In essence, you are saying that you are limiting risk by filtering each investment for a high reward-to-risk ratio. Then you are trying to capture the best moves in the price action of the market by concentrating efforts in those few areas that are trending. Is that correct?

DF: Yes. Certain sectors pull the market up or down. These sectors change regularly. By putting dollars into sectors that are not leading, I tend to have more risk without the upside. The mere fact that these sectors are not in trend with the broad market tells me that there is nothing leading these stocks where I expect them to go.

RL: Uncertainty translates to risk.

DF: Always.

Reward and Risk

RL: What is your minimum acceptable reward-to-risk ratio?

DF: I look at anything that gives me at least a 2:1 ratio. I don't look at anything that is 1:1 regardless of other factors.

RL: What advantages are there to having the skills of an active trader in your longer-term investing and asset management?

DF: The skills that I have as a trader have helped immensely. The approach to my investing, I believe, would still be far better than most simply because of my methodology, but having the skills to really define my entries and exits adds tremendously to my performance.

RL: Would you say that someone interested in actively overseeing his or her own investments would benefit from the kind of technical analysis and trade management that is employed by more active traders?

DF: Without a doubt. I think the knowledge and skill brought to the table by someone with training as a trader is huge. An example of that would be . . . once a decision to purchase a stock is made using a daily chart, I will go down to an hourly or five-minute chart to find an optimal price to purchase. With some simple technical analysis I can better define where support is and where a reasonable area to enter the trade might be.

RL: Can you give any other specific examples of how your trading skills affect your investing?

DF: Position sizing. Knowing how much to invest is often as important as knowing where to invest. Though people can spend years learning the art of position sizing, understanding the basics can have an immediate impact on portfolio performance.

FUNDAMENTAL ANALYSIS

RL: We haven't talked much about fundamental analysis. How important is that to you?

DF: To be honest, I have found fundamental analysis to be less and less important over the years. I have become more and more disillusioned. Fundamental analysis can provide such a cloudy picture, while technical analysis tends to be very clear. It is nice to have a story behind the trade, but technicals [technical analyses] get me into the trade and technicals get me out of the trade.

RL: Do you maintain a long-term view on a particular stock or currency that helps guide your investment decision?

DF: Generally, I do have an opinion about the long-term outlook for a currency or stock, but I don't let it affect my risk management. In other words, if a position that I am holding breaks support, I sell it—regardless of my long-term view.

I can always get back into a trade if it gets back into its trend. I have no problem getting out and then getting back in later. I keep more of my capital, and I sleep better at night.

Money Management

RL: What is the best way for a trader or an investor to tell how he or she is performing?

DF: There are a variety of financial measurements that should be used as review metrics by anyone serious about the performance of his or her portfolio. Things like the Kelly ratio, the Sortino ratio, and the Sharpe ratio can give an accurate risk-adjusted picture of a portfolio's performance. Though they are hardly used by the average investor, they should be a standard for everyone.

Below are the ratios referred to by Dave Floyd along with some practical explanation on where they are most useful:

KELLY RATIO. The Kelly ratio or formula is used by money managers to assist in the process of deciding what percentage of allocations to make to specific investments. If you risk too little, your money won't grow; and if you risk too much, the drawdowns will put you out of business. In between too little and too much risk is where capital can find its maximum potential.

The original Kelly formula was developed back in 1956 by J. L. Kelly, who was working with AT&T Bell Labs to solve problems involving random interference on telephone lines. What Kelly discovered was a method for increasing data flow while reducing random information loss. In the investment world, this same reasoning allows us to mathematically figure proper portfolio percentages to invest in various styles or strategies.

SHARPE RATIO. This ratio was developed by Bill Sharpe to measure risk-adjusted performance. It is calculated by subtracting the risk-free rate of

return (what you might expect from a money-market account) for a portfolio and dividing the result by the standard deviation (a measure of how much
volatility the portfolio endures) of the portfolio returns. The Sharpe ratio is
designed to give a mathematical measurement of a portfolio's performance
as it is related to the risk that it takes. It lets us know whether the results of
performance are a result of a smart investing style or a result of excess risk.

SORTINO RATIO. This ratio is often considered a variation of the Sharpe
ratio. Essentially, the Sortino ratio uses the same formula, except it uses the
downside deviation for the denominator where the Sharpe uses the standard
deviation. This means that the Sortino takes out the volatility associated
with upside performance and looks only at the downside volatility.

RL: What is the secret to longevity as a trader or investor? How do you
consistently meet and beat your goals?

DF: The secret is no more complicated than the secret for losing weight.
The problem is people don't do it. Actively seeking out good opportunities while maintaining consistent risk management is the key. You
can't use risk management sometimes and not others. It has to be
something you do all the time. This is really all it takes to build significant wealth over time.

In managing mutual fund and stock portfolios, we often use what we
call a *style box analysis model* (*SBAM*), which helps us to identify those
sectors that are beginning a parabolic move up and those sectors that are
beginning a parabolic move down. We are able to change those portfolios
so that they are generally following the trends of sectors moving in the most
favorable uptrend. In portfolios where—through the use of options, shorting, or inversely correlated investments—we are able to take advantage of
sectors moving down we also take advantage of those sectors beginning a
downward trend. (See Exhibit 9–4.)

The concept of floating investments in and out of sectors as they ebb
and flow is not a new concept, but it has not yet become accepted as a standard of practice or design in the mutual fund industry. Maybe it is because
of the close ties investment banking firms maintain with their publicly

Industry Sector Style Box

Utilities	Oil and Gas	Retail Apparel	Biotech	Financial Services	Retail Specialty
Communi-cations Service	Aerospace Defense	Major Pharma	Food Services	Software and Program	Education
Regional Banks	Computer Hardware	Communi-cations Equip	Forestry and Wood Product	Consumer Non-cyclical	Waste Mgmnt
Insurance	Chemical Mfr	Computer Services	Health-care Svcs	Metal Mining	Medical Equip
Airlines	Auto and Truck Mfr	Semi-conductor	Transpor-tation	Gold and Silver	Broad-casting
Real Estate	Entertain-ment	Home Builders	Consumer Cyclical	Hotel Motel	Casinos Gaming

EXHIBIT 9-4

traded clients, or perhaps the rational is simply that it takes too much effort to be active managers. Regardless of the reason, the results are the same: a largely antiquated and ineffective set of tools.

What we have grown to know as diversification still holds some utility, but it doesn't compare to the long-term efficacy found in diversification across styles and time horizons. The concept of diversification across styles and time frames has given rise to a number of very successful alternative investment funds. Many of these are in the form of hedge funds. Though they don't fit the normal constructs of what we consider "funds" and they are generally not used as a hedge against anything, hedge funds are rapidly growing in popularity around the globe.

These funds gravitate in two directions. The first is referred to as a fund of hedge funds, or more succinctly a fund of funds (see also Chapter 6). The manager of a fund of funds is responsible for finding individual hedge funds that work synergistically to provide a consistent return and relatively low risk. The idea behind the fund of funds is similar to that of a mutual fund, but the manager blends hedge funds rather than individual equities.

The second is a multistrategy fund (see also Chapter 6). The management of a multistrategy fund tends to have most if not all of its managers working exclusively for the fund, or it has the same management team directing multiple strategies. Both formats have proved to be very effective. Their popularity has spread in part in response to the demand by investors and institutions for active management and diversification of hedge fund investments. Since hedge fund strategies vary from the very broad to the very specific, fund of fund managers provide an invaluable service. The charge of each manager is more than just to bring added performance over time through synergistic combinations of funds. It is also to reduce relative risk through the efficient matching of strategies. And when combining strategies or managers that value absolute return, that value diversification across styles and time, and that have the ability to get it done, you are on the right track.

Diversification is a great method for smoothing out the performance of your portfolio. What Wall Street has lost in common sense, it has made up for in tenacity. There is logic to diversification that must be asserted for it to truly work. There is nothing that proves the ineffectiveness of today's most renowned diversification models like a real bear market.

If you have seen your portfolio fall with the markets, then you can appreciate the gaps in the commonly accepted principles of diversification. They have just not held up under the scrutiny of time or the market. As is often the case with theory, scientific or otherwise, reality brings out the deficiencies over time. Regrettably the model that was championed in the 1950s by Harry Markowitz has not been followed in the spirit in which it was created. When Markowitz's Nobel Prize–winning theory on diversification was first introduced, investments in international markets were quickly adapted as part of a well-diversified portfolio. After all, the relationship of the international markets to that of the United States and others was minimal.

Over 50 years of steady growth in the capital markets has brought countries closer together. The correlation of the capital markets in Europe, Asia, and Latin America has become increasingly close. So much so, that international investing is no longer a simple way to diversify a portfolio. But it is still considered one of the basic tenets of good diversification. The concept of maintaining a portfolio weighted across asset classes was clarified by Markowitz in his original works to include the need to hold assets that have little relationship to one another. Wall Street has forgotten that the devil is in the details.

Regrettably, the diversification model that has become a standard now for decades has proved defective. If it were all that were available, then we would have to learn to accept the risks that millions had no idea existed until more recent times. There is, however, a better way. The real-life efficacy of these principles is evidence that must not be dismissed by any serious investor.

10

Markets Are Efficient

I recognize that the efficient market hypothesis is a Nobel Prize–winning theory, but after more than 20 years of studying and trading stocks, options, commodities, and futures, my response was and continues to be "You have got to be kidding!" Like thousands of others around the world, I earn a living from the inefficiencies in the market, not the efficiencies. The collaborative efforts of the finance and economic departments at universities in the United States and Europe are unequivocally the most prolific in the world. The advances that have been made because of the likes of Merton, Scholes, Black, Markowitz, Bernstein, Friedman, and others in just the last century have been as revolutionary as the first conceptualizations of the number zero.

The efficient market hypothesis, though intriguing and thought-provoking, is without practical merit. This may explain in part why the buy-and-hold theory has also foundered in practice. The idea that markets will continue to fluctuate around an upward-trending mean is supported by hundreds of years of data that appear graphically to show a slightly choppy but upward-trending market. The reasons to expect markets to continue moving up over time include the improved value of the marketplace created by innovation and invention, the growing population of persons on the planet participating in the promotion of growth and value in the marketplace, and long-term inflation. As we discussed in the Chapter 3 on buy and hold, the time required to mitigate the volatility of crashes like the ones we have seen multiple times in just the past century is prohibitively long.

Of course the efficient market hypothesis is not dependent upon markets trending in any direction. It is merely the platform used by brokers and advisers to herald the certainty of rising markets. In taking a macro-to-micro view of the marketplace, I could make the assumption that better health care, better medicines, and even natural selection are increasing life expectancy. Additionally, I could assume that with the slow and steady increase in the population of the United States, the geriatric population will likely become more and more significant. From these assumptions, I may conclude that investing in health care services, nursing homes, and alternative care facilities is only logical. But there is absolutely no guarantee that the market will respond in an efficient manner. If the market would respond efficiently, these sectors would move slowly upward over time, with each individual price being affected only by those things relative to the real value of the stock. Price would move only in response to data like sales and earnings. But that is simply not the case. Not only does price fail to account for these kinds of performance data, but oftentimes price moves completely counter to the information.

During the Internet boom of the 1990s, I remember countless occasions where companies announced that they had missed their earnings expectations by a wide margin, only to see the price of the stock shoot skyward on the news. Aggressive buyers took every opportunity to buy stocks on dips for any reason because a runaway bull market dominated their macro view. If the markets had been more efficient, the price action of stocks would have been considerably smoother.

The efficient market hypothesis is predicated upon everyone getting the same information at the same time. First, let's wrangle with the idea that everyone gets the same information. This shouldn't take long. The quantity of information made available is so voluminous that no one—and I mean no one—could possibly take it all in. From the *Wall Street Journal*, *Financial Times*, and *Barron's* to the thousands of newsletters and online services—not to mention CNN, CNBC, and Bloomberg—anyone could be easily overwhelmed. The information varies in its content from paper to paper, from service to service, and from station to station. Continuity of information and its dissemination is all but nonexistent. It is ridiculous to think that all people have access to the same information. It is even more ludicrous to think that anyone could take it all in if it were available.

We have all heard the saying "Perception is everything." Well, it is no truer than in the world of finance. Supposing every person did receive the same information from the same sources, there is still the problem of perception. If you have never played the game Telephone, you should give it a try sometime. You will be surprised at what you learn. The purpose of the game is to see if a sentence or two can be told to one person and then repeated by that person to another and another through a group of 10 or 12 people while maintaining the integrity of the message. Played best in a circle, it never fails to get giggles once the message makes its way back to its originator. Sentences that began as "Betty wants to go to the beach" end up as "Beds and sinks are within reach." The reason is that people hear things differently, and they interpret what they hear differently. What would you expect? We are only human.

Perceptions are as diverse as personalities. Since it is scientifically impossible for all people to interpret information in exactly the same fashion, it can be logically concluded that individuals maintaining diverse market perspectives and having dissimilar backgrounds and investment motives will react disparately. Plus perception has little to do with being right or wrong. Investors finding value in a stock that has dropped precipitously may not fully understand the reason for the fall. Their resultant buying may drive prices up, at least temporarily, but with no change in the real value of the company. In the mid-1990s, news of an Internet company missing its earnings targets met with a drop in price that lasted only a few minutes at most before it would begin rocketing skyward again. Some mistakenly perceived that poor performance would draw sellers to the market. It didn't. No one was selling. Buy high and sell higher was the rule of the day. Three years later corporate earnings reports that beat estimates were regularly greeted with an immediate sell-off. Times change, just as perceptions change. It does not happen in an instant. Most often the process is a gradual one, and one that is as imperfect as it is inefficient.

News is like a child growing up—it happens whether we are there or not (Moral: Spend time with your kids. They do grow up). There is no mechanism in place to assure us that information will be made available at the same time to everyone. Consequently, we all get our information from various sources and at various time intervals. In my office, I have a Bloomberg terminal that regularly gives breaking news and real-time economic reports minutes ahead of other more mainstream media. This allows my trading desk to enter the market ahead of the pack. This is just one example of the inefficiencies of markets. In this case the inefficiency helps me to get into positions where I may profit in only a few minutes from the delay that others endure wittingly or unwittingly. Though some may say that such inefficiencies create an unequal and unfair advantage, I would contend that the two should be separated. Admittedly, while my more efficient method for accessing data puts me on a playing field that is unequal, it is most certainly not unfair. Mr. Bloomberg will gladly sell his service to anyone who is willing to pay for it, but most people either cannot or will not. For an investor holding funds for months or years, breaking news will play a minuscule part in improving efficiency. For the investor or trader with a shorter time horizon, the tool is often considered invaluable. This is just one example of the inefficiencies of markets. While many markets have themselves improved their efficiencies, there are barriers to true efficiency that may never be overcome. The cost to maintain a Bloomberg terminal, for example, is generally prohibitive for the nonprofessional; and to make use of such a tool would require that one spend a significant amount of time at or near the terminal.

As a fund manager, I have a time horizon that is different from that of other managers in the firm. Some are shorter, and some are longer. I also use technical analysis to determine stop-loss points. These price points are set to define and limit the amount of risk that any position in the portfolio will bear. For a short-term or swing-trading style, a stop loss may be pennies, whereas the long-term manager may have risk parameters set in dollars. Since both are looking at the same information with different perspectives, they tend to react differently.

Strategy is also a dynamic affecting market efficiencies. One of the beautiful things about the financial markets of the world is the shear breadth of opportunity they hold for investors and traders. Countless strategies exist because there are boundless ways to view the markets. Similar strategies do not guarantee that the execution of those strategies will be the same. There are just too many variables. Minor differences in entry points, exit points, risk management, order-entry technique, number of shares purchased or sold, and much more can be attributed to the entry into and the impact on the market. Even buy-and-hold strategies are built on a plethora of esoteric perspectives that result in buying (and even the occasional selling to buy something better) at different times and price points. Under the strong form of the efficient market hypothesis, this evidence should also prove challenging.

In light of the fact that performance of funds with very similar design can see deviations of 18+ percent over any five-year period, the selection of fund managers may be more important than previously thought. (See Exhibit 10–1.)

Mutual Fund Performance Variances

Fund Name	Symbol	1-Year Return	3-Year Return	5-Year Return	10-Year Return
AIM Global Health Care A	GGHCX	26.08%	1.81%	7.29%	13.38%
ASAF Invesco Health Sciences A	INHAX	21.70%	2.61%		
Alliance Bernsteing Health Care A	AHLAX	18.32%	26.00%		
Eaton Vance Worldwide Health Sci A	ETHSX	26.98%	2.88%	15.97%	17.82%
Fidelity Advisor Health Care A	FACDX	11.35%	-1.92%	0.79%	
Franklin Global Health Care A	FKGHX	26.59%	-3.38%	6.65%	9.38%
Invesco Advantage Health Sci A	IAGHX	19.39%	-0.92%	-1.25%	10.87%
Janus Global Life Sciences A	JAGLX	34.64%	2.17%	10.13%	
Jennison Health Sciences A	PHLAX	46.31%	8.06%		
John Hancock Health Sciences A	JHGRX	24.36%	3.29%	5.52%	12.13%
Merrill Lynch Healthcare A	MDHCX	16.96%	1.68%	6.68%	

(continued)

EXHIBIT 10-1

Fund Name	Symbol	1-Year Return	3-Year Return	5-Year Return	10-Year Return
Morgan Stanley Health Sciences A	HCRAX	29.78%	4.77%	10.99%	
Munder Healthcare A	MFHAX	58.46%	2.75%	17.16%	
Putnam Health Sciences A	PHSTAX	11.42%	-2.56%	0.20%	12.58%
State Street Research Health Sci A	SHSAX	63.64%	15.67%		
T. Rowe Price Healths Sciences	PRHSX	43.43%	10.80%	10.84%	
Vanguard Health Care	VGHCX	32.45%	6.80%	12.41%	

Notes:

Derived from http://finance.yahoo.com.
Returns adjusted for loads.

Points:

1. Performance varies—a lot!

2. Not many major firms have long-running funds. Most have started new funds and depend on name for marketing.

3. You don't always have to pay a premium to get the best. Firms like Vanguard and T. Rowe have no loads that do better than the rest.

4. Specialty funds may have much more volatility than a hedged fund. Many funds with a focus on health sciences have had drawdowns in excess of 50%.

5. Having been around doesn't mean smarter management. State Street is "a perfect example."

EXHIBIT 10-1 (continued)

Like new renditions of old classics, the notes may be the same, but the sound is entirely novel. Had markets proved to be truly efficient, there would be little need for dozens of managers in each sector of the market. It seems a bit ironic that the same firms that preach the values of efficient markets are still able to tell clients that their funds are somehow better designed than those of other firms. Equally ironic is the size of the salaries paid to fund managers when the expected return is nothing more than the benchmark of the S&P, the Dow Jones Industrial Average, the NASDAQ 100, or the Russell 2000. If little chance of actually beating the general performance of a sector over time exists, then the buy-and-hold investor would do better to buy and hold the exchange-traded fund or index described in Chapter 5.

To find out what a prospective manager does to achieve his or her results, call, write, or e-mail the firm or the manager. You may even want to listen in on the regularly scheduled conference calls held by many firms. If you cannot find the evidence to support this manager's effort to provide effective active management with goals of absolute returns, then don't invest.

Summary

W all Street is under attack, and for good reason. An investor revolution has been a long time coming. Major financial firms supported by ivory tower researchers with no practical aptitude have perpetuated veritable myths unchallenged for decades. As this book is being penned, investors are witnessing the growing pains of this financial revolution.

I expect the results will be nothing short of wondrous, though they will not occur overnight. Along with freedom and knowledge come responsibility and accountability. In a paradigm shift of this magnitude there is a heightened propensity for investors to modify their mind-set before checking the appropriate emotions and acquiring adequate knowledge. For example, the advent of direct-access trading platforms has opened most markets to the individual investor. Mutual funds, stocks, bonds, futures, options, and even foreign currencies can now be traded electronically. Increased efficiencies have reduced commission expense and made short-term trading quite practical. It must be said, however, that low transaction costs and direct market access have only finite benefits, while market knowledge and its practical application have infinite value.

Even if you're on the right track,
you'll get run over if you just sit there.
—WILL ROGERS

HOW YOU CAN GET IT RIGHT

The first step in taking command of your financial future is to fully understand what you want and how you might obtain it. Know that you can achieve high absolute returns unfettered by the limitations of traditional Wall Street managers. Part of this freedom comes from rejecting the notion that securities markets are highly efficient. There is no need to accept the small incremental returns tied to market averages when there is abundant opportunity for creating wealth from the inefficiencies that exist. Change your perception of risk such that it becomes a cost of business that you control while continually working to improve margins and enhance profitability. Be flexible, and open to opportunity. Design your financial goals so that they are dynamic enough to address risk and seize opportunity quickly. Most importantly, remember that preservation of capital is the key to future wealth creation.

Now find a financial adviser who knows the difference between Wall Street rhetoric and real-life performance. Also make sure that you have an adviser who customizes your financial plan to fit your individual goals and objectives. Interview prospective advisers so that you can be confident that they will be recommending an investment portfolio that makes use of diversification among truly noncorrelated investments that are not burdened with high front-end-load fees or penalties for early withdrawal. One way to make sure a prospective adviser is concerned with the absolute returns on your portfolio is to clarify what metrics he or she uses to measure performance. If indications are that the adviser looks only at beating major indexes, then look for the nearest exit. On the other hand, the adviser who professes an absolute-return focus should still be examined further. Ask how he or she actively manages a portfolio to achieve desired returns. To what extent are mutual fund strategies utilized? Are they incorporated into a type of "wrap" account where there are no extra fees for moving in and out of funds, or are ETFs the vehicle of choice? How does the adviser approach market cycles? Determine whether extended bear markets will be met with high cash, money-market, or bond reserves or whether the adviser's style rotates into other markets, industries, or investments that may be noncorrelated or inversely correlated to the broad market indexes. More experienced money managers will tend to have a selection of at least five or ten subadvisers or alternative managers from which to choose.

Financial planning grows more complex as time passes. The planner or adviser who is well versed in estate planning and insurance will typically defer asset management efforts to a subadviser whose entire focus is the active management of a portfolio, or in some instances a portion of a portfolio. Firms that have established relationships with subadvisers are often able to put you, the investor, in front of high-quality asset managers without any additional fees. Look for this type of efficiency from your adviser.

The next step in building and maintaining wealth is creating a comprehensive plan for financial growth. For the plan to be truly comprehensive, it should include goals, strategies, and contingencies while remaining dynamic to account for changing markets, changing goals, and new opportunities. Your adviser should include "rally points" or instances where you both should reconvene based on predetermined events. These rally points may represent events where additional preparation is required—such as after the birth of a child or on the diagnosis of Alzheimer's of a parent or grandparent. Events such as these require that you as an investor notify your adviser. Other rally points, such as a change in tax law or the maturing of a note, are generally called by the adviser. Establish the rules for getting together, with a minimum default amount of one year. Regardless of the market or your place in life, your adviser will want to at least confirm that all things are working as planned. It is empowering to know conclusively where your investments stand and how they will be changed or modified as the future unfolds.

BECOMING AN EXPERT

Getting the plan in place is a great accomplishment, but it is only the beginning if you intend to maximize your endeavors. Schedule a time on your own to review your investments to ascertain how each is performing. If you keep a journal to make a brief record of your assessments, you will begin to get a feel for each of the markets where your investments are active. Make it a point to learn. Start by splitting your efforts between financial matters where you have great interest and financial matters where you feel you are weak. Your confidence will swell, and your finances will benefit. Though you may really like real estate and have had success in buying rental properties, you may find that multiunit complexes are conducive to your lifestyle or investing goals. Interestingly, the reason many investors don't make investments in specific funds or projects is not so much because they don't like the project as it is they lack understanding. Learning about foreign currency trading might open your eyes to an interesting investment area with risk-reward ratios that you never imagined could exist. Studying the new methods in geologic research may clarify what methods are most reliable for finding and drilling for oil. You may also decide that investing in single stocks is too volatile and time-consuming and that investing in sector funds is more suited to your personality. Whether you attend seminars regularly or put together a reading schedule, get the knowledge.

LEAVING A LEGACY OF WEALTH

Regardless of your faith, human nature pushes us toward something bigger than ourselves. We are on this planet for a relatively short period of time, should all history now and later be considered. In this time we have an opportunity to leave the earth and the people in it better than when we arrived. You might say we are driven to leave a legacy. My mother counts the hundreds of students she has taught over four decades and knows that their lives and their children's lives may be affected by the lessons she imparted. My father, a real estate developer, drives by town centers and restaurants with visible pride, as he knows the people there are enjoying themselves as a result of his efforts. My pastor weeps as he sees people walking down the aisle with hearts turned toward God, knowing that eternity for them will be different. Each of us has been blessed with assets, many we probably don't even know we have. If we are to leave a legacy that will have a lasting impact, we should begin planning for it now. Start by thinking "Wouldn't it be great if . . . ," and then fill in the blank. And fill it in again—and again—and again. Is it giving our children a better family life than we had, or a better education? Perhaps, helping to build a new school or sponsoring a chair in science at our alma mater is a great calling. It might be paying off the farm and creating a trust so that our family heritage will be preserved, or maybe it is just spending quality time with loved ones in our retirement.

    Whether you want to build a zoo or sponsor missionaries around the globe, you are the steward of your assets. Remember the cliché "No one cares about your money as much as you do"? Well, no one is accountable for reaching your goals but you either. Your broker's retirement is not linked to how he performs for you, and the market has a mind of its own. Grab the reins, and make your portfolio work for you.

Key Terms

VALUABLE FINANCIAL TERMS AND RATIOS

ACID-TEST RATIO: The ratio used to measure a company's liquidity and evaluate creditworthiness. It is found by taking current assets minus inventories, accruals, and prepaid items to liabilities.

ADVANCE-DECLINE LINE: A market analysis tool used to measure the overall market's direction. Equal to the number of stocks that rose divided by the number of stocks that fell during some specified period.

ALPHA: A measure of risk-adjusted performance considering the risk of the specific security rather than the overall market.

ARBITRAGE: A strategy of buying a security or commodity in one market and selling it in a different market.

BETA: A quantitative measure of the volatility of a given stock, mutual fund, or portfolio, relative to the overall market, using a benchmark like the S&P 500. A beta above 1 is more volatile than the overall market, while a beta below 1 is less volatile.

r-SQUARED: A measurement of how closely a portfolio's performance correlates with the performance of a benchmark index, such as the S&P 500, and thus a measurement of what portion of its performance can be explained by the performance of the overall market or index. Values for *r*-squared range from 0 to 1, where 0 indicates no correlation and 1 indicates perfect correlation.

RESISTANCE: Inability of a stock to rise above a certain price (resistance level).

SHARPE RATIO: Named after Nobel laureate economist and Financial Engines founder William F. Sharpe, a ratio designed to measure an investment's return relative to its risk. To calculate a fund's Sharpe ratio, you divide the fund's returns in excess of the risk-free rate (e.g., the 90-day Treasury bill rate) by its standard deviation. If a fund produced a return of 5 percent with a standard deviation of 10 percent while the T-bill returned 5 percent, its Sharpe ratio would equal 0.

SLIPPAGE: The difference between estimated and actual transaction costs.

SORTINO RATIO: A variation of the Sharpe ratio which differentiates harmful volatility from volatility in general using a value for downside deviation. The Sortino ratio is the excess return over the risk-free rate over the downside semivariance, and so it measures the return to "bad" volatility. This ratio allows investors to assess risk in a better manner than simply looking at excess returns to total volatility, since such a measure does not consider how often the price of the security rises as opposed to how often it falls.

STANDARD DEVIATION: A statistic that illustrates how closely all the various points of data are clustered around the mean in a sample of data. When the examples are fairly tightly bunched together and the bell-shaped curve is steep, the standard deviation is small. When the examples are spread apart and the bell curve is relatively flat, the standard deviation is relatively large. A standard deviation can give you an idea of how much the performance varies from time period to time period. Though a low standard deviation is often considered good, the measure is more one of consistency than of proficiency. An investment that consistently loses 10 percent per month could have a standard deviation of zero.

SUPPORT: In technical analysis, a price level that a security has had difficulty falling below.

MODELS AND THEORIES

BLACK-SCHOLES OPTION PRICING MODEL: A model used to calculate the value of an option, by considering the stock price, the strike price, the expiration date, the risk-free return, and the standard deviation of the stock's return.

CAPITAL ASSET PRICING MODEL (CAPM): An economic model for valuing stocks by relating risk and expected return. The model is based on the idea that investors demand additional expected return (called the risk premium) if asked to accept additional risk.

DIVIDEND GROWTH MODEL: A model wherein dividends are assumed to be growing at a constant rate in perpetuity. The value of the stock equals next year's dividends divided by the difference between the required rate of return and the assumed constant growth rate in dividends.

EFFICIENT FRONTIER: The combination of investments that maximizes expected return for any level of expected risk or that minimizes expected risk for any level of expected return.

EFFICIENT PORTFOLIO: A portfolio that provides the greatest expected return for a given level of risk (i.e., standard deviation) or, equivalently, the lowest risk for a given expected return.

GOLD STANDARD: Essentially an international monetary system in which currencies are defined in terms of their gold content and payment imbalances between countries are settled in gold.

KEYNESIAN ECONOMICS: The doctrine established by John Maynard Keynes suggesting that active government intervention in the marketplace and monetary policy at key times is the best method of reducing the risk of financial instability in the investment markets and in the economy as a whole.

ARBITRAGE PRICING THEORY (APT): An alternative asset pricing model to the capital asset pricing model. Unlike the capital asset pricing model, which specifies returns as a linear function of only systematic risk, arbitrage pricing theory may specify returns as a linear function of more than a single factor.

DOW THEORY: Technical theory that a major trend in the stock market must be confirmed by simultaneous movement of the Dow Jones Industrial Average and the Dow Jones Transportation Average to new highs or lows.

EFFICIENT MARKET THEORY: A theory, though largely discredited now, that argues that all market participants receive and act on all the relevant information as soon as it becomes available. If this were strictly true, no investment strategy would be better than a coin toss. Proponents of the efficient market theory believe that there is perfect information in the stock market. This means that whatever information is available about a stock to one investor is available to all investors (except, of course, insider information, but insider trading is illegal). Since everyone has the same information about a stock, the price of a stock should reflect the knowledge and expectations of all investors. The bottom line is that an investor should not be able to beat the market since there is no way for him or her to know something about a stock that isn't already reflected in the stock's price. Proponents of this theory do not try to pick stocks that are going to be winners; instead they simply try to match the market's performance. However, there is ample evidence to dispute the basic claims of this theory, and most investors don't believe it.

MODERN PORTFOLIO THEORY (MPT): An overall investment strategy that seeks to construct an optimal portfolio by considering the relationship between risk and return, especially as measured by alpha, beta, and r-squared. This theory recommends that the risk of a particular stock should not be evaluated on a stand-alone basis, but rather in light of how that particular stock's price varies in relation to the variation in price of the market portfolio. The theory goes on to state that given an investor's preferred level of risk, a particular portfolio can be constructed that maximizes expected return for that level of risk. MPT is also called modern investment theory.

RANDOM WALK THEORY: An investment theory that claims that market prices follow a random path up and down, without any influence by past price movements, making it impossible to predict with any accuracy which direction the market will move at any point. In other words, the theory claims that the path a stock's price follows is a random walk that cannot be determined from historical price information, especially in the short term. Investors who believe in the random walk theory feel that it is impossible to outperform the market without taking on additional risk, and they believe that neither fundamental analysis nor technical analysis has any validity. However, some proponents of this theory do acknowledge that markets move gradually upward in the long run.

APPROACHES TO THE MARKET

ACTIVE PORTFOLIO MANAGEMENT: A money-management strategy based on an independent investment decision which seeks to match the performance of the overall market (or some part of it) by mirroring its composition or by being broadly diversified. The opposite is passive management, or indexing.

BOTTOM UP: An investment strategy in which companies are considered based simply on their own merit, without regard for the sectors they are part of or the current economic conditions. A person following this strategy will be looking very closely at the company's management, history, business model, growth prospects, and other company characteristics. He or she will not be considering general industry and economic trends and then extrapolating them to the specific company. Followers of this strategy believe that some companies are superior to their peer groups and will therefore outperform regardless of industry and economic circumstances. The object of bottom-up investing is to identify such companies. Opposite of top down.

BUY-AND-HOLD STRATEGY: A strategy that calls for accumulating shares in a company over years. This is a long-term investment strategy with not a lot of active trading.

DOLLAR COST AVERAGING: An investment strategy that involves investing a fixed amount in a particular investment at regular intervals, such as putting $500 into a particular stock or fund each month. The amount you invest remains constant, so you purchase more shares when the price is low and fewer shares when the price is higher. This method of investing is also called a constant-dollar plan.

LADDER PORTFOLIO STRATEGY: A bond portfolio strategy in which the portfolio is constructed to have approximately equal amounts invested in every maturity/redemption rate within a given price range.

SECTOR ROTATION: The movement of money by one investor or the over-all market from one or more sectors into one or more other sectors. Also called rotation.

TOP DOWN: An investment strategy that first finds the best sectors or industries to invest in and then searches for the best companies within those sectors or industries. This investing strategy begins with a look at the over-all economic picture and then narrows it down to sectors, industries, and companies that are expected to perform well. Analysis of the fundamentals of a given security is the final step. Opposite of bottom up.

PROFESSIONAL DESIGNATIONS

ACCREDITED ASSET MANAGEMENT SPECIALIST (AAMS): A desig-nation awarded by the College for Financial Planning upon completion of a 12-module study program and a comprehensive final exam.

AAMFA FELLOW: Chartered Wealth Manager (CWM), Chartered Asset Manager (CAM), Master Financial Professional (MFP), Chartered Trust and Estate Planner (CTEP).

All these designations are awarded by the American Academy of Finan-cial Management for persons meeting standards for education, testing, ethics, experience, and continued education. AAMFA focuses on individu-als, such as brokers, investment advisers, or trust officers, who manage money for high-value customers.

ACCREDITED ESTATE PLANNER (AEP): A credential awarded by the National Association of Estate Planners and Councils to estate planning practitioners who complete a comprehensive exam grounded in the subjects of trusts, insurance, accounting, and law.

CERTIFIED FINANCIAL PLANNER (CFP): A title conveyed by the Inter-national Board of Standards and Practices for Certified Financial Planners. A certified financial planner must pass a series of exams and enroll in ongo-ing education classes. Knowledge of estate planning, tax preparation, insur-ance, and investing is required.

CHARTERED FINANCIAL ANALYST (CFA): An individual who has passed tests in economics, accounting, security analysis, and money management, administered by the Institute of Chartered Financial Analysts of the Association for Investment Management and Research. Such an individual is also expected to have at least three years of investments-related experience and meet certain standards of professional conduct. These individuals have an extensive economic and investing background and are competent at a high level of analysis.

CHARTERED FINANCIAL CONSULTANT (ChFC): A financial planning designation for the insurance industry awarded by the American College in Bryn Mawr, Pennsylvania. ChFCs must meet experience requirements and pass exams covering finance and investing. They must have at least three years of experience in the financial industry, and they must have studied and passed an examination on the fundamentals of financial planning, including income tax, insurance, and investment and estate planning. Corporations utilize their services as security analysts, portfolio managers, and investment advisers.

CHARTERED LIFE UNDERWRITER (CLU): A designation granted by the American College in Bryn Mawr, Pennsylvania, to individuals who have completed training in life insurance and personal insurance planning. To obtain the designation, individuals have to complete advanced courses and exams in several topics including insurance, investments, taxation, employee benefits, estate planning, accounting, management, and economics.

REGISTERED INVESTMENT ADVISER (RIA): A person or organization employed by an individual or mutual fund to manage assets or provide investment advice. Also called a financial adviser or investment adviser or investment counsel. Often spelled advisor.

Glossary

ALL OR NONE ORDER A limited price order for an investment given to a broker that states the order is to be executed in its entirety or not at all (no partial transaction).

ANALYST An employee of a brokerage or mutual fund company who studies various companies and makes buy and sell recommendations on the stocks of these companies. Most specialize in a specific industry or sector.

ANNUITY A contract sold by an insurance company to a policyholder or by a pension plan to participants that makes regular periodic payment for a specified period of time. These are usually low risk and safe investments for individuals.

ARBITRAGEUR A person who attempts to profit from the price differences of stocks, currency, or commodities that are traded on two or more market exchanges.

AT THE MONEY (ATM) A condition in which the strike price of an option is equal to (or nearly equal to) the market price of the underlying security.

BACK-END LOAD MUTUAL FUND A sales charge or commission paid when an individual sells a mutual fund or an annuity. This is used to discourage early withdrawal of the fund.

BALANCED MUTUAL FUND A mutual fund that buys both stocks and bonds. A balanced mutual fund is more diversified, thus reducing investors' risk exposure to the market.

BASIS POINT A measurement unit used to describe differences between yields or interest rates. For example, 25 basis points equals .25% or one-quarter of one percent.

BENCHMARK A standard used by investors to compare performance. For instance, a large-cap growth mutual fund may use the S&P 500 performance as its benchmark.

BONDS A debt instrument issued for a period of more than one year with the purpose of raising capital by borrowing. The federal government, states, cities, corporations, and many other types of institutions sell bonds. Generally, a bond is a promise to repay the principal along with interest (coupons) on a specified date (maturity). Some bonds do not pay interest, but all bonds require a repayment of principal. When an investor buys a bond, the investor becomes a creditor of the issuer. However, the buyer does not gain any kind of ownership rights to the issuer, unlike in the case of equities. On the other hand, a bond holder has a greater claim on an issuer's income than a shareholder in the case of financial distress (this is true for all creditors). Bonds are often divided into different categories based on tax status, credit quality, issuer type, maturity, and secured or unsecured (and there are several other ways to classify bonds as well). U.S. Treasury bonds are generally considered the safest unsecured bonds, since the possibility of the Treasury defaulting on payments is almost zero. The yield from a bond is made up of three components: coupon interest, capital gains, and interest on interest (if a bond pays no coupon interest, the only yield will be capital gains). A bond might be sold at above or below par (the amount paid out at maturity), but the market price will approach par value as the bond approaches maturity. A riskier bond has to provide a higher payout to compensate for that additional risk. Some bonds are tax-exempt. These are typically issued by municipal, county, or state governments, whose interest payments are not subject to federal income tax, and sometimes also state or local income tax.

BRADY BONDS Bonds that are issued by the governments of developing countries. Brady Bonds are some of the most liquid emerging market securities. They are named after former U.S. Treasury Secretary Nicholas

Brady, who sponsored the effort to restructure emerging market debt instruments. The price movement of Brady Bonds provides an accurate indication of market sentiment toward developing nations. Most issuers are Latin American countries.

CALL OPTION A type of option contract that gives its holder the right (but not the obligation) to buy a specified number of shares of the underlying stock at the given price, on or before the expiration date of the contract.

CALL PREMIUM The amount that the buyer of a call option has to pay to the seller for this right to purchase a stock or stock index at a specified price by a specific date.

CAPITALIZATION A company's stock price per share multiplied by the total number of shares outstanding. Also known as *market cap*.

CHINESE WALL This is a slang term derived from the "Great Wall of China" to describe the barrier within a brokerage firm that is designed to prevent insider information from being handed out by corporate advisers to the trading desk. The Chinese Wall helps prevent illegal practices such as front running by traders. Established after the crash of 1929, the U.S. government sought to provide a separation between investment bankers and brokerage firms. It has come under fire in recent years as questions have arisen as to the conflict of interest that exists between analysts' objective research and the desire to have a successful stock offering (IPO).

CLOSED-END ETF Like a traditional mutual fund, a Closed-End ETF is an investment company that pools the assets of its investors and uses professional managers to invest the money to meet clearly identified objectives, such as current income or capital appreciation. However, unlike a mutual fund, a Closed-End ETF issues a fixed number of shares through an initial public offering, and lists those shares on a national stock exchange such as the New York Stock Exchange (NYSE) or the American Stock Exchange (AMEX). Investors who wish to buy or sell fund shares do not purchase or redeem directly from the fund—rather, they buy or sell fund shares on the stock exchange in a process identical to the purchase or sale of any other listed stock.

The price of a Closed-End ETF typically resembles, but is independent of, the underlying net-asset-value of the fund. When demand for fund shares exceeds supply, the market price at which a Closed-End ETF trades may be higher than its underlying net-asset-value. When there are more fund sellers than buyers, the market price may be lower than its net-asset-value. Closed-End ETFs may also use leverage to enhance returns by borrowing capital using debt securities or through the issuance of preferred shares.

CLOSED-END MUTUAL FUND A type of fund that has a fixed number of shares. These funds do not readily issue and redeem shares on a regular basis, unlike open-ended funds.

COLLAR A combination of put options and call options that can limit, but not eliminate, the risk that their value will decrease.

COMMODITY A physical substance, such as food, grains, and metals, which is interchangeable with another product of the same type, and which investors buy or sell, usually through futures contracts. The price of the commodity is subject to supply and demand. Risk is actually the reason that exchange trading of basic agricultural products began. An example might be a farmer who is at risk for producing a product with an expectation of a future sales price but at risk for that sales price changing before the product can be produced and sold. The farmer may elect to sell a contract guaranteeing delivery at a prespecified price to lock in his profits.

CORRELATION A measure sometimes given as a "correlation coefficient" that describes a complementary or parallel relationship between two securities. For example, the performance of two stocks within the same industry or sector is generally highly correlated. Investors typically seek styles and/ or strategies that have low correlations to one another as a means of reducing portfolio risk and volatility.

COVERED CALL The process of selling a call option while at the same time holding an equivalent position in the original security.

COVERED OPTION An option contract backed by the shares of the original option. The two types are covered call and covered put.

CRASH An abrupt drop in market prices or economic conditions.

DELTA The change in the price of a buyer's right to purchase a given amount of stock at a specific price (option contract) in relation to the change in the price of the stock.

DERIVATIVE A financial instrument whose characteristics and value depend upon the characteristics and value of the underlying, typically a commodity, bond, equity, or currency. Examples of derivatives include futures and options. Advanced investors sometimes purchase or sell derivatives to manage the risk associated with the underlying security, to protect against fluctuations in value, or to profit from periods of inactivity or decline. These techniques can be quite complicated and quite risky.

DIVERSIFICATION Dividing investment funds among a variety of securities with different risk and reward profiles or expectations. Diversification has changed over recent decades to mean noncorrelated investments reflecting varying strategies, time frames, and risk profiles.

EARNINGS PER SHARE A company's profit divided by its number of outstanding shares. If a company earned $2 million in one year and had 2 million shares of stock outstanding, its EPS would be $1 per share.

EMERGING MARKET STOCKS Stocks of companies based in nations with developing economies.

EXCHANGE TRADED FUND (ETF) A fund that tracks an index, but can be traded like a stock on major exchanges. All of the major stock indexes have ETFs based on them, including the Dow Jones Industrial Average, the Standard & Poor's 500 Index, and the Nasdaq Composite.

EXERCISE PRICE The price at which the security underlying a future or options contract may be bought or sold.

EXPENSE RATIO The percentage of the assets that were spent to run a mutual fund (as of the last annual statement). This includes expenses such as management and advisory fees and overhead costs.

FEDERAL FUNDS RATE The interest rate that banks with excess reserves at a Federal Reserve district bank charge other banks that need overnight loans.

FEDERAL RESERVE SYSTEM   The central bank of the United States, established in 1913, and governed by the Federal Reserve Board located in Washington, D.C. The system includes 12 federal reserve banks and is authorized to regulate monetary policy in the United States as well as to supervise federal reserve member banks, bank holding companies, international operations of U.S. banks, and U.S. operations of foreign banks.

FIVE "Cs" OF CREDIT   Five characteristics that are used to form a judgment about a customer's creditworthiness: character, capacity, capital, collateral, and conditions.

FUNDAMENTAL ANALYSIS   A method of security valuation that involves examining a company's financials and operations, especially sales, earnings, growth potential, assets, debt, management, products, and competition. Fundamental analysis takes into consideration only those variables that are directly related to the company itself, rather than the overall state of the market or technical analysis data.

FUTURES CONTRACT   An agreement to buy or sell a set amount of financial instruments or physical commodities on a designated future date at a price agreed upon today by the buyer and seller.

FUTURES MARKET   A market in which contracts for future delivery of financial instruments or physical commodities are bought and sold.

GLOBAL FUNDS   Mutual funds that can invest anywhere in the world, including the United States.

GOLD STANDARD   An international monetary system in which currencies are defined in terms of their gold content, and payment imbalances between countries are settled in gold.

HEDGE FUND   A fund, usually used by wealthy individuals and institutions, which is allowed to use aggressive strategies that are unavailable to mutual funds, including selling short, leverage, program trading, swaps, arbitrage, and derivatives. Hedge funds are exempt from many of the rules and regulations governing other mutual funds, allowing them to accomplish aggressive investing goals. They are restricted by law to no more than 100 investors per fund, and as a result most hedge funds set extremely high minimum investment amounts, ranging anywhere from $250,000 to over $1 million. As with traditional mutual funds, investors in hedge funds pay a management fee; however, hedge funds also collect a percentage of the profits (usually 20 percent).

HIDDEN LOAD A type of sales charge or transactional fee that is charged to an investor, often without their knowledge, such as a mutual fund 12b-1 fee.

IMPLIED VOLATILITY A theoretical value designed to represent the volatility of the security underlying an option as determined by the price of the option. The factors that affect implied volatility are the exercise price, the risk-less rate of return, maturity date, and the price of the option. Implied volatility appears in several option pricing models, including the Black-Scholes Option Pricing Model.

INITIAL PUBLIC OFFERING (IPO) A company's first sale of stock to the public.

INTERNATIONAL MONETARY FUND (IMF) An organization founded to oversee currency exchange arrangements of member countries and to lend foreign currency reserves to members with short-term balance of payment problems or to developing countries.

INTERNATIONAL MUTUAL FUND As a rule of thumb, a fund labeled "international" will buy primarily foreign securities—companies outside the United States. There are several types. A "regional" international fund concentrates on markets in one part of the world. "Emerging market" international funds focus on developing countries and the securities listed on exchanges in those countries.

IN THE MONEY (ITM) A situation in which an option's strike price is below the current market price of the underlying (for a call option) or above the current market price of the underlying (for a put option). Such an option has intrinsic value.

INTRINSIC VALUE The amount by which an option is in the money, calculated by taking the difference between the strike price and the market price of the underlying.

LIMIT ORDER An order to buy a stock at or below a specified price or to sell a stock at or above a specified price.

LOAD FUND A mutual fund with shares sold at a price including a sales charge—typically 4 to 8 percent of the net amount.

LONG BONDS Bonds with a long current maturity. The best known is the 30-year U.S. Treasury bond.

LONG POSITION When an investor who has the right, but not the obligation, to buy or sell bonds, or shares of stock or mutual funds, at a set price on or before a given date, has bought, and now owns, more contracts than he's sold over a specific length of time.

MARRIED PUT The purchase of a put option on a stock that is already owned. A married put protects against a decline in the price of the underlying stock. If the price declines, the stock can be sold at the higher price anytime before expiration. Of course, if the stock price remains neutral or increases, the option is worthless and the premium is lost.

NATIONAL ASSOCIATION OF SECURITIES DEALERS (NASD) A nonprofit organization of people who directly participate in the buying and selling of stock in the over-the-counter market, where, instead of meeting on an exchange floor, geographically dispersed dealers are linked together by telephones and computer screens. Nasdaq is the best-known over-the-counter market.

NATIONAL ASSOCIATION OF SECURITIES DEALERS AUTOMATIC QUOTATION (NASDAQ) An electronic quotation system that provides price quotations to market participants about the more actively traded common stock issues in the O.T.C. market. About 4000 common stock issues are included in the Nasdaq system.

NEW YORK STOCK EXCHANGE (NYSE) The largest market for the buying and selling of stocks. To be eligible for listing on the NYSE, a company must earn at least $2,500,000 a year (before taxes), have issued at least 1,000,000 shares of stock, and give voting rights to common stockholders.

NO LOAD MUTUAL FUND A mutual fund with shares that are sold without a sales charge.

NOTE An investment instrument, such as a bond, with maturities greater than one year and less than ten years.

NOTIONAL FUNDING In certain trading strategies where leverage is a standard of practice, firms will consider funding that is not in the account for purposes of measuring risk and reward. For example, a manager who only uses $25,000 of a $100,000 account may allow investors to put in $25 to $50,000. Notional funding can be a double-edged sword as gains and losses are both magnified.

OPEN-END FUND A mutual fund that continually offers it shares for purchase by investors. Investors redeem open-end fund shares by selling them back to the fund. This practice is in contrast to closed-end funds and other exchange-traded securities, which are bought and sold by investors in the open markets.

OPTIMAL PORTFOLIO A portfolio that maximizes an investor's preferences with an ideal balance of returns and risk.

OPTION CONTRACT The right, but not the obligation, to buy (for a call option) or sell (for a put option) a specific amount of a given stock, commodity, currency, index, or debt, at a specified price (the strike price) during a specified period of time. For stock options, the amount is usually 100 shares. Each option has a buyer, called the holder, and a seller, known as the writer. If the option contract is exercised, the writer is responsible for fulfilling the terms of the contract by delivering the shares to the appropriate party. In the case of a security that cannot be delivered, such as an index, the contract is settled in cash. For the holder, the potential loss is limited to the price paid to acquire the option. When an option is not exercised, it expires. No shares change hands and the money spent to purchase the option is lost. For the buyer, the upside is unlimited. Options, like stocks, are therefore said to have an asymmetrical payoff pattern. For the writer, the potential loss is unlimited unless the contract is covered, meaning that the writer already owns the security underlying the option. Options are most frequently used as either leverage or protection. As leverage, options allow the holder to control equity in a limited capacity for a fraction of what the shares would cost. The difference can be invested elsewhere until the option is exercised. As protection, options can guard against price fluctuations in the near term because they provide the right to acquire the underlying stock at a fixed price for a limited time. Risk is limited to the option premium (except when writing options for a security that is not already owned). However, the costs of trading options (including both commissions and the bid/ask spread) is higher on a percentage basis than trading the underlying stock. In addition, options are very complex and require a great deal of observation and maintenance.

OPTIONS CONTRACT A contract that, for a premium price, gives an investor the right to buy or sell a stock at a set price on or before a specific date.

OUT OF THE MONEY (OTM) A call option whose strike price is higher than the market price of the underlying security, or a put option whose strike price is lower than the market price of the underlying security.

OVER-THE-COUNTER (OTC) A securities market where geographically dispersed dealers are linked together by telephones and computer screens, trading for securities not listed on a stock or bond exchange, such as the New York Stock Exchange. The Nasdaq market is the best-known OTC market.

OVERSUBSCRIBED ISSUE This occurs when a new issue of securities is underpriced or in great demand because of growth prospects, and investors are not able to buy all the shares they'd like to.

PAR Equal to the nominal or face value of an investment instrument, such as a bond. A bond selling at "par," for instance, is worth an amount equivalent to its original issue value or its value upon redemption at maturity.

P/E EFFECT Traditionally, portfolios with low P/E stocks have exhibited higher average risk-adjusted returns than high P/E stocks.

PENNY STOCK Stock that typically sells for less than $1 a share. Usually, these stocks are offered over the counter or on regional stock exchanges.

PENSION BENEFIT GUARANTY CORPORATION (PBGC) A federal agency that insures the vested benefits of pension plan participants. The PBGC was established in 1974 by ERISA legislation.

PREFERENCE STOCK A type of stock that ranks junior to preferred stock but senior to common stock in the right to receive dividend payments from the firm.

PREFERRED SHARES Preferred shares give investors a fixed dividend from the company's earnings. And more importantly: preferred shareholders get paid dividends before common shareholders. If the company is liquidated, preferred shareholders are paid their claim on company assets before common shareholders are. Like common stock, preferred stocks represent partial ownership in a company, although preferred stock shareholders do not enjoy any of the voting rights of common stockholders. Also unlike common stock, a preferred stock pays a fixed dividend that does not fluctuate, although the company does not have to pay this dividend if it lacks the financial ability to do so. The main benefit to owning preferred stock is that the investor has a greater claim on the company's assets than common stockholders. Preferred shareholders always receive their dividends first and, in the event the company goes bankrupt, preferred shareholders are paid off before common stockholders. In general, there are four different types of preferred stock: cumulative preferred, non-cumulative, participating, and convertible. These are also called *preference shares*.

PREMIUM The amount that the buyer of an option pays to the seller.

PRICE VALUE OF A BASIS POINT A measure of the change in the price of a bond if the required yield changes by one basis point, or yield percentage. For example, an interest rate of 5 percent is 50 basis points greater than an interest rate of 4.5 percent.

PRICE/BOOK RATIO This compares the price at which a stock is trading and presumably could be sold to the value of total assets less total liabilities (book value). This ratio is determined by dividing current stock price by common stockholder equity per share (book value), adjusted for stock splits.

PRICE/EARNINGS RATIO Also known as P/E. P/E shows the "multiple" of earnings at which a stock sells. The P/E is determined by dividing current stock price by current earnings per share (adjusted for stock splits). Earnings per share for the P/E ratio are often determined by dividing earnings for the past 12 months by the number of common shares outstanding. Higher "multiple" means investors have higher expectations for future growth, and have bid up the stock's price.

PRIMARY MARKET The first buyer of a newly issued security buys that security in the primary market, such as in an Initial Public Offering. All subsequent trading of those securities is done in the secondary market, such as on stock exchanges.

PROGRAM TRADING Trades based on signals from computer programs, usually entered directly from the trader's computer to the market's computer system and executed automatically.

PROSPECTUS A formal written document to sell securities that describes the business plan for an existing or proposed company that an investor needs in order to make an informed decision. Prospectuses also are used for mutual funds to describe the fund objectives, risks, and other essential information.

PUBLIC OFFERING An offering of a company's stock usually made by an investment banker or a syndicate made up of several investment bankers, at a price agreed upon between the issuer and the investment bankers. See also Initial Public Offering (IPO).

PUT OPTION An option granting the right to sell a set number of shares of a specific stock in a designated future month at a price agreed upon today by the buyer and seller. Buyers of put options bet the stock's price will go down below the price set by the option.

RED HERRING A preliminary prospectus containing information about a company that intends to issue stock.

REDEMPTION CHARGE A charge imposed on a mutual fund when redeeming shares within a certain period of time after purchase. For example, a 2 percent redemption charge on the sale of shares valued at $1000 will result in a payment to the investor of $980 (or 98 percent of the value).

REFUNDED BOND Also called a pre-refunded bond, one that originally may have been issued as a general obligation or revenue bond but that is now secured by an "escrow fund" consisting entirely of direct U.S. government obligations that are sufficient for paying the bondholders.

REGIONAL STOCK EXCHANGES Securities exchanges located outside of New York City and registered with the S.E.C. They include: Boston, Cincinnati, Intermountain (Salt Lake City—dormant, owned by COMEX), Midwest (Chicago), Pacific (Los Angeles and San Francisco), Philadelphia

(Philadelphia and Miami), and Spokane (local mining and Canadian issues, nonreporting trades).

RESTRICTED STOCK Stock that is granted subject to specified conditions on the stockholder's ability to sell or borrow against the shares. As a general rule, these condition, or restrictions, lapse at a future date or upon the occurrence of specified events.

REVERSE STOCK SPLIT A proportionate decrease in the number of shares, but not the total value of shares of stock held by shareholders. Shareholders maintain the same percentage of equity as before the split. For example, a 1-for-3 split would result in stockholders owning 1 share for every 3 shares owned before the split. After the reverse split, the firm's stock price is, in this example, worth three times the pre-reverse split price. A firm generally institutes a reverse split to boost its stock's market price.

ROLL OVER When an investor reinvests funds received from a maturing security, such as a bond or a money-market certificate, in a new issue of the same or a similar security.

ROUND LOT A trading order typically of 100 shares of a stock or some multiple of 100.

RULE OF 72 The estimation of doubling time on an investment, where the compounded annual rate of return times the number of years must equal roughly 72 for the investment to double in value.

SECONDARY ISSUE Sale of already issued stock.

SECONDARY MARKET The market where securities are traded after they are initially offered in the primary market, such as through Initial Public Offerings. Most trading is done in the secondary market. The New York Stock Exchange, as well as all other stock exchanges, the bond markets, etc., are secondary markets.

SECTOR A distinct subset of a market, society, industry, or economy, whose components share similar characteristics. Stocks are often grouped into different sectors depending upon the company's business. Standard & Poor's breaks the market into 11 sectors. Two of these sectors, utilities and consumer staples, are said to be defensive sectors, while the rest tend to be more cyclical in nature. The other nine sectors are: transportation, technology, health care, financial, energy, consumer cyclicals, basic materials, capital goods, and communications services. Other groups break up the market into different sector categorizations, and sometimes break them down further into sub-sectors.

SECURITIES & EXCHANGE COMMISSION (SEC) A federal agency that regulates the U.S. financial markets and also oversees the securities industry.

SELLING SHORT If an investor thinks the price of a stock is going down, the investor could borrow the stock from a broker and sell it. Eventually, the investor must buy the stock back on the open market. For instance, say you borrow 1000 shares of XYZ on July 1 and sell it for $8 per share. Then, on August 1, you purchase 1000 shares of XYZ at $7 per share. You've made $1000 (less commissions and other fees) by selling short.

SHORT A term describing a person who has sold a contract to establish a market position and who has not yet closed out this position through an offsetting purchase.

SHORT BONDS Bonds with minimal time periods until they mature.

SHORT POSITION This occurs when a person sells stocks he or she does not yet own. Shares must be borrowed, before the sale, to make "good delivery" to the buyer. Eventually, the shares must be bought back to close out the transaction. This technique is used when an investor believes the stock price will go down.

SPDRs (SPIDERS) SPDRs are designed to track the value of the Standard & Poor's 500 Composite Price Index. They are known as *Spiders*. SPDRs is short for Standard & Poor's Depositary Receipt. One SPDR unit is valued at approximately one tenth (1/10) of the value of the S&P 500.

SPLIT Sometimes companies split their outstanding shares into a larger number of shares. If a company with 1 million shares did a two-for-one split, the company would have 2 million shares. An investor with 100 shares before the split would hold 200 shares after the split. The investor's percentage of ownership in the company remains the same, and the price of the stock he owns is one-half the price of the stock on the day prior to the split.

SPOT INTEREST RATE The interest rate fixed today on a loan that is made today.

SPOT MARKETS Markets that involve the immediate delivery of a security or instrument to a purchaser.

SPREAD The gap between the highest price an investor is willing to pay to buy a security and the lowest price an investor will accept to sell a stock.

STANDARD & POOR'S 500 (S&P 500) A market-weighted index of leading stocks, in which the total market value of each stock gives a corresponding weight to its mathematical importance in computing the index. For example, the price of a stock with a market cap of $10 billion will be given twice the weight, or importance, of a stock of a company with a market cap of $5 billion.

STANDARD DEVIATION A statistical measure of the degree that a value in a probability distribution varies from the mean of the distribution; a measure of how far a value can deviate from the statistical mean.

STOCK Ownership of a corporation, which is represented by shares that represent a piece of the corporation's assets and earnings.

STOP ORDER An order to buy or sell at the market when a definite price is reached, either above (on a buy) or below (on a sell) the per-share price in effect when the order was given.

STOP-LIMIT ORDER A stop order that designates a price threshold to buy a stock at or below a specified price or to sell a stock at or above a specified price.

STOP-LOSS ORDER An order to sell a stock when the price falls to a specified level.

STRADDLE The purchase or sale of an equal number of puts and calls, with the same strike price and expiration dates. A straddle provides the opportunity to profit from a prediction about the future volatility of the market. Long straddles are used to profit from high volatility. Long straddles can be effective when an investor is confident that a stock price will change dramatically, but cannot predict the direction of the move. Short straddles represent the opposite prediction: that a stock price will not change.

STRANGLE An options strategy involving a put option and a call option with the same expiration dates and strike prices that are out of the money. The investor profits only if the underlying moves dramatically in either direction.

STRIKE PRICE The stated price per share for which underlying stock may be purchased (in the case of a call) or sold (in the case of a put) by the option holder upon exercise of the option contract that gives the buyer the right to buy or sell shares of a stock at a set price on or before a given date.

STYLE ANALYSIS A technique for evaluating your portfolio by comparing its historical return to that achieved by a set of basic investment categories called asset classes (such as cash, bonds, large-cap, and so forth.) Style analysis focuses on how a fund behaves, not on what the fund currently owns.

TAX SWAP Exchanging two similar bonds to receive a tax benefit.

TECHNICAL ANALYSIS A method of evaluating securities by relying on the assumption that market data, such as charts of price, volume, and open interest, can help predict future (usually short-term) market trends. Unlike fundamental analysis, the intrinsic value of the security is not considered. Technical analysts believe that they can accurately predict the future price of a stock by looking at its historical prices and other trading variables. Technical analysis assumes that market psychology influences trading in a way that enables predicting when a stock will rise or fall. For that reason, many technical analysts are also market timers, who believe that technical analysis can be applied just as easily to the market as a whole as to an individual stock.

TIME VALUE OF AN OPTION The portion of an option's premium that is based on the amount of time remaining until the expiration date of the option contract, based on the concept that the underlying components that determine the value of the option may change during that time.

TOMBSTONE An advertisement listing the underwriters of a stock—the party or parties that guarantee proceeds to the firm from a sale of its stock.

TREASURY (U.S. DEPARTMENT OF) The branch of the U.S. government that issues Treasury bonds, notes, and bills.

TREASURY BILLS Debt obligations of the U.S. Treasury that have maturities of 1 year or less. Maturities for T-bills are usually 91 days, 182 days, or 52 weeks.

TREASURY BONDS Debt obligations of the U.S. Treasury that have 10 years or more until they expire.

TREASURY NOTES Debt obligations of the U.S. Treasury that expire in more than 2 years but less than 10 years.

TRIPLE WITCHING The four times a year when the Standard & Poor's (S&P) futures contract expires at the same time as the S&P 100 index option contract and option contracts on individual stocks. This occurs on the third Friday of March, June, September, and December.

TURNOVER A measure of trading activity in a specific mutual fund during a period of time, expressed as a percentage of the average total portfolio value of the fund. A turnover ratio of 25 percent means that the value of trades represented one-fourth of the fund's investments.

UNCOVERED OPTION A call option written (uncovered call) or a put option purchased (uncovered put) without ownership of the underlying asset. Also called a *naked option*.

UNDERWRITE To guarantee a company a specific price for its stock by entering into an agreement to purchase the stock at that price. Investment banks frequently do this when a company issues a new block of stock.

UNIT INVESTMENT TRUST A structure used by some ETFs. One important difference between this format and the open-end fund format is that the latter allows ETFs to reinvest dividends immediately, while the former does not. This could result in ETFs that use the unit investment trust structure having a slight cash drag on their performance.

VOLATILITY A numerical measure of the risk of a company's stock due to its historic price fluctuations, as compared with the stock market as a whole, or with other stocks in the industries in which it does business.

It also refers to the relative rate at which the price of a security moves up and down. Volatility is found by calculating the annualized standard deviation of daily change in price. If the price of a stock moves up and down rapidly over short time periods, it has high volatility. If the price almost never changes, it has low volatility.

WINDOW DRESSING Slang for trading activity near the end of a quarter or fiscal year that is designed to "dress up" a portfolio to make it look attractive to shareholders or clients. For example, a portfolio manager may sell losing positions in a portfolio so they can display only positions that have gained in value.

WORLD BANK A multinational company that makes loans to developing countries for social overhead capital projects, such as the building of an electrical power grid to a rural area. These loans are guaranteed by the country that receives them.

WRAP ACCOUNT A variety of investment services typically including investment advice, brokerage, and custody, which are provided by a financial services firm to a customer for one set fee. The services are combined together, or "wrapped."

WRITER The seller of an option, usually an individual, bank, or company, that confers the right to buy or sell stock at a given date at a certain price.

X OR XD A frequently used symbol in many U.S. newspapers which indicates that a stock is traded without a dividend.

Index

About the Author

RICHARD L. LACKEY is the CEO and managing partner of ETS Capital Management, which manages assets for institutions and high-net-worth individuals, as well as president of ETS Financial Services, a trader training firm. A nationally recognized authority on trading and investing, Lackey has more than two decades of experience trading equities, options, futures, and currencies. He is a popular speaker at investment seminars and conferences, and appears regularly in national broadcast and print media.